GREAT GRAINS

LINDA DRACHMAN

AND

PETER WYNNE

In consultation with Lynne Hill, R.D.

A JOHN BOSWELL ASSOCIATES/
KING HILL PRODUCTIONS BOOK

A Fireside Book
Published by Simon & Schuster

New York London Toronto Sydney
Tokyo Singapore

ACKNOWLEDGMENTS

To my husband, Frank, daughter, Leigh, and son, David, for their unfaltering support, encouragement and confidence.

Special thanks to Susan Wyler, for her clear vision, thoroughness, impeccable taste and guidance from inception to completion of this book.

A John Boswell Associates/King Hill Productions Book

Fireside
Simon & Schuster Building
Rockefeller Center
1230 Avenue of the Americas
New York, NY 10020

FIRESIDE and colophon
are registered trademarks
of Simon & Schuster, Inc.

Design by Nan Jernigan/The Colman Press

Printed and bound in the United States of America

1 3 5 7 9 10 8 6 4 2

Library of Congress Cataloging-in-Publication Data

Drachman, Linda.
Great Grains/by Linda Drachman and Debra Rosman.
    p.   cm.—(Feed your family right)
"A John Boswell Associates/King Hill Productions book."
"A Fireside book."
ISBN 0-671-72899-7: $9.95
1. Cookery (Cereals)   I. Rosman, Debra.   II. Title.   III. Series.
TX808.D73   1991
641.6'31—dc20   90–24204
                                              CIP

CONTENTS

The grain that feeds America comes in many forms. Here are exciting recipes for wheat in all its guises: *Roast Chicken and Bulgur with Oregano Yogurt Dressing, Gazpacho-Couscous Salad, Curried Cracked Wheat and Shrimp Salad, Whole Wheat Applesauce Waffles,* and *Super Duper Tuna Pasta Salad.*

It's more American than apple pie and comes in two basic forms: fresh sweet corn and dried cornmeal. This superb collection of recipes covers them both, with dishes like *Slim Steak Stir-Fry with Baby Corn and Snow Peas, Chicken Pozole, Cranberry Corn Bread,* and *Baked Polenta with Chunky Tomato Sauce.*

They're tasty and nutritious and much more than just a breakfast cereal. Expand your oat horizons with ideas like *Twice-Baked Walnut Oat Cookies, Apple Cranberry Crisp with Crunchy Oat Topping, Crispy Deviled Chicken Drumsticks,* and *Marvelous Meat Loaf, made extra nutritious with oats and lean ground turkey.*

Two dozen ways to prepare the world's most popular grain, including white rice, brown rice, wild rice and specialty varieties. These nutritionally balanced recipes include *Stir-Fried Chicken with Rice and Peanuts, Risotto with Fresh Peas, Turkey Tofu Chili with Brown Rice,* and *Apricot and Pecan Brown Rice.*

INTRODUCTION: GRAINS AND GOOD HEALTH

Good health and good nutrition are inseparable, and a practical way to get started on both is to begin eating more grains. Tiny but potent bits of nutrition, grains offer the things health experts say we should include in our daily diet: protein, fiber, carbohydrates, vitamins and minerals. At the same time, grains are low in the things most of us should avoid. They have little saturated fat and, like all foods coming from plants, no cholesterol whatever.

Putting more grain into our daily diet is a matter of getting back to basics. In this day of highly refined and processed foods, most of the grains we eat are in forms that bear little resemblance to their sources. Each year, for example, Americans consume more than 100 pounds of wheat per person, but nearly all of it goes into commercially baked goods, pasta and flour for use at home.

Grains are seeds, mostly from what are called "cereal grasses." These include barley, corn, millet, oats, rice, rye and wheat. Although different from each other in use, flavor and food value, all the cereal grains have much in common. As far as cooks and nutritionists are concerned, the kernels of cereal grains are made up of three parts:

▲ **BRAN:** These are the highly nutritious outside layers that surround and protect the kernel. Bran is rich in vitamins and minerals and contains most of the dietary fiber found in grains.
▲ **GERM:** This is the part of the seed that would grow if the kernel were planted. Like the bran, the germ is particularly rich in vitamins and minerals.
▲ **ENDOSPERM:** This is the largest part of the kernel, often more than 80 percent of its weight. Mostly starches, but with some protein, the endosperm is the food supply that sustains a grain plant during its first weeks of life.

The kernels of cereal grains are usually enclosed in hulls that must be threshed away because they're inedible. A handful of grains come from plants that aren't grasses, among them buckwheat and the less familiar amaranth and quinoa (pronounced "keen-WAH"). With these, the hulls are sometimes eaten with the grain. This is true of amaranth and quinoa, although not buckwheat.

Grains from grasses and nongrasses also differ somewhat in the amino acids that make up their respective proteins, a fact important to vegetarians, but mostly the two types share more similarities than not.

Whether they come from cereal grasses or other kinds of plants, grain and grain products provide significant amounts of good-quality protein; thiamin, riboflavin, niacin and other B vitamins; minerals such as iron, phosphorus, magnesium and zinc; food energy derived chiefly from starches and other complex carbohydrates, and most of the dietary fiber that Americans consume on a regular basis.

Nutritionists say we should eat four servings of grain or grain products daily and that a single serving could be a muffin or a thick slice of bread; ½ to ¾ cup of cooked macaroni or noodles; the same size portion of cooked rice, barley, bulgur, grits or hot cereal; or 1 ounce of a dry cereal.

In the kitchen, grains offer wonderful possibilities, starting with breakfast and going right through the day. All grains can be cooked and eaten as hot breakfast cereals.

As the day progresses, whole and cracked grains, which have longer cooking times, come into their own as ingredients in salads, stews and casseroles, as additions to baked goods and as stuffings for vegetables, poultry and fish.

With *Great Grains,* we hope to provide the user a "cook's tour" of the wonderful world of grains. This book offers more than 120 delicious and healthful ways to get more grains into today's diet, including an entire chapter devoted to recipes for children. "For Finicky Eaters" tells how to make grain-rich muffins, soups and other dishes that will have the kids clamoring happily to eat healthily.

NUTRITIONAL GUIDELINES

In recent years, many health organizations have made strong recommendations about the American diet. What seems to be common to all of them are the five following general principles of healthy eating for adults and older children.

▲ Achieve and maintain desirable body weight.
▲ Eat a nutritionally adequate diet consisting of a variety of foods.
▲ Reduce consumption of fat, especially saturated fats, and cholesterol.
▲ Increase consumption of complex carbohydrates and fiber.
▲ Reduce sodium intake.

Following are the specific nutritional guidelines that relate to these principles:

CALORIES — A measure of the energy available to the body from any food. The ideal daily caloric intake varies significantly depending upon age, sex, body type and activity level. It is the number of calories it takes to maintain your ideal weight. An average adult woman, for example, might need 1,500 calories a day to maintain her weight, while a large, active man might require 2,400 a day; persons trying to lose weight might have to restrict themselves to a mere 1,200 calories.

PROTEIN — Made of amino acids, the "building blocks" of the body, protein is essential to allow growth and repair of cells and to maintain optimum body functions. As important as it is, most Americans consume far more protein, and consequently more calories and often more cholesterol and saturated fats, than they need. Protein has 4 calories per gram, and it is recommended that only 15 to 20 percent of your daily calories come from protein.

TOTAL FATS — Fats provide the most concentrated source of calories at 9 calories per gram. Although the body needs a small amount of fat for energy and to help absorb oil-soluble vitamins, most of us eat far more fat than we need. Calories from all fats should be limited to no more than 30 percent of the calories ingested in a day. The following table relates fat intake to calories following this 30 percent guideline.

Daily Calories	Total Fat Maximum	Saturated Fat Maximum
	gm	gm
2,400	80	26
2,000	66	22
1,800	60	20
1,500	50	16
1,200	40	13
1,000	33	11

(Recommendations are according to the American Dietetic Association, the American Heart Association and the National Cancer Institute.)

SATURATED FATS — Saturated fats are found in foods from animals, such as meat, poultry and eggs, in whole-milk dairy products and butter, and in palm oil, palm kernel oil and coconut oil, often used in processed foods. Product labeling can be misleading, because while a food might be touted as having no cholesterol, it may contain one of these saturated fats, which also tend to raise the blood cholesterol level. It is the total nutritional profile of a product or recipe that counts. Intake of saturated fats should be limited to no more than 10 percent of daily calories (see chart above).

CHOLESTEROL — Dietary cholesterol is found only in foods from animal sources. Our own bodies also manufacture cholesterol. There is strong medical evidence that reducing the intake of cholesterol and fats, especially saturated fats, helps to lower cholesterol levels in the blood. An average healthy adult should eat no more than 300 milligrams of cholesterol a day.

CARBOHYDRATES — These are the sugars and starches that provide our bodies with energy and dietary fiber. Simple sugars, which we get from foods like cookies, candies and sweeteners, are quickly digested and pass into the bloodstream, where they boost the blood sugar level, which then falls off rapidly. They offer little more than energy. Complex carbohydrates usually include starches, which may contain vitamins, minerals, fiber and some protein. They are broken down more gradually and assimilated slower, so that blood sugar levels remain more stable. We get complex carbohydrates from fruits, vegetables and grains, and most Americans need to add more of these to their diet. Carbohydrates contain 4 calories per gram, and it is recommended that they comprise 50 to 60 percent of our daily calories.

SODIUM — Sodium is found naturally in many foods; in balance with potassium, it helps regulate cell integrity and is linked to blood pressure. Excess sodium intake provides no known benefit and in some people may be linked to high blood pressure and cardiovascular disease. Consequently, the National Research Council of the National Academy of Sciences recommends that even healthy adults limit their sodium intake to a maximum of 2,400 milligrams a day, while the American Heart Association allows up to 3,000.

DIETARY FIBER — This is the structural part of plants also known as "roughage" or "bulk." There are two different kinds of fiber — soluble, which can be digested, and insoluble, which passes through the digestive system largely untouched. Fiber helps prevent constipation, aids in stabilizing blood sugar levels in diabetics, may prevent certain types of cancer and has been shown to help lower blood cholesterol levels when used in conjunction with a low-fat diet. Recommended levels of fiber are 20 to 35 grams per day.

As appealing as a healthy diet sounds and as simple as these prescribed guidelines appear at first glance, they are often confusing, because the percentages given are on a daily basis, which makes them difficult to utilize meal by meal, especially since actual recommended amounts vary dramatically depending on sex, age, weight and body type.

In general, the best way to eat a healthier diet is to change your eating habits to include more complex carbohydrates and less saturated fats and sodium. The following recipes, each with its own nutritional breakdown of calories, protein, total fat, saturated fat, cholesterol, carbohydrates, sodium, and dietary fiber, have been customized to assure healthy eating.

Many of the recipes are packed with vitamins and minerals, as well. Whenever a recipe contains over 20 percent of the U.S. Recommended Daily Allowance of a valuable vitamin or mineral, we've highlighted it on a bar graph below. Recipes that are not as high in these particular nutrients are also included because they contain a healthful balance of protein, fats and carbohydrates for the number of calories, and they are low in sodium and cholesterol.

The recipes in this book all come in at no more than 525 calories; all but a few are below 500. They allow a maximum of 800 milligrams of sodium and 125 milligrams of cholesterol; most contain much less. Except where otherwise noted, all calorie and other nutritional counts are per serving. Where an odd number of servings, such as 5, is listed, the recipe could serve a range, from 4 to 6. Nutritional counts have been rounded off to the nearest whole number.

Lynne Hill, R.D.

NEW WAYS WITH WHEAT

Wheat and wheat products include some of the tastiest, most nutritious and low-cost foods we have. Per capita consumption of wheat in this country is more than 100 pounds a year, with most of it going into pasta, commercial baked goods and flours that are used at home. That brief list, however, gives little hint of the remarkable number of forms wheat can take, including wheat berries, cracked wheat, bran (see "A Bran Bonanza," p. 92), wheat germ, semolina, farina, bulgur, pasta and four or five kinds of flour. Together, these provide the cook nearly endless possibilities.

Wheat germ, the growing part of the wheat seed, is removed from grain destined to become white flour. The germ has a rich, nutty taste, but contains oil that can go stale and give flour an off flavor. In recent years, however, we've come to realize that we shouldn't overlook the germ, where so much of the vitamin and mineral content of the wheat seed is concentrated. Thus wheat germ is now sold as a food item across the land.

Wheat germ can be used to give a nutritional boost to all kinds of foods. It can be added to meat loaf and burgers, substituted for part of the flour in breads and cookies and sprinkled over cereal, salads and even ice cream. Wheat germ can also be used as breading for chicken and fish, as Chicken Nuggets with Sweet-and-Sour Dipping Sauce will deliciously demonstrate. Whatever way it's used, wheat germ is best stored in the refrigerator.

Wheat berries are wheat kernels with the inedible hulls removed. They can be sprouted for use in salads and baked products; they can be cooked and eaten as a breakfast cereal, used in salads or added to meat loaf and hamburgers. Our Zucchini Wheat Berry Bars, with cinnamon and other sweet spices, should convince even the skeptics that good nutrition and good flavor can go hand in hand.

Cracked wheat is prepared by breaking wheat berries into small pieces. It can be cooked and eaten as a hot cereal or added uncooked to baked goods to provide a nutty flavor and crunchy texture.

Semolina is a granular meal made from the endosperm, or starchy portion, of durum wheat, which is a different species from the wheats used for breads and cakes. Pasta manufacturers use semolina to make top-quality spaghetti and macaroni.

Flours are milled with their use in mind:

▲ **Bread flour** has a high percentage of protein, including gluten, which is a sticky, elastic substance that gives bread a light, springy texture and a certain chewiness.

▲ **Cake flour** has a greater percentage of starch, which keeps cakes and pastries tender and delicate.

▲ **All-purpose flour** tries to strike a balance by including enough gluten to give bread a good rise but not so much that it toughens cakes and pastries.

The flours mentioned so far are all made of wheat kernels from which the bran and germ have been removed.

▲ **Whole wheat or graham flour** is milled from entire wheat kernels and includes the fiber-rich bran and nutritious germ.

Our Very Light Whole Wheat Bread combines whole wheat and bread flours with rolled oats to give a loaf that's both light in texture and hearty in flavor. Whole Wheat Pita and our Whole Wheat Applesauce Waffles show two other sides of this flavorful, versatile flour.

Bulgur is a processed form of cracked wheat. The whole grain is parboiled; about 5 percent of the bran is removed; then the grain is dried and cracked. Our Roast Chicken and Bulgur with Oregano Yogurt Dressing, and Tabbouleh are two flavorful ways to bring this Middle Eastern favorite to your dinner table.

The grainlike couscous of North Africa, Sicily and elsewhere is a kind of instant pasta that's cooked like a grain. Preparing old-fashioned couscous was something of a production, involving repeated steaming and fluffing the granules of semolina. Most of the couscous on the market today is a quick-cooking variety that has been precooked and dried. For an exotic treat, try our Couscous with Lamb and Slivered Almonds, our Tomatoes Stuffed with Minted Couscous, or our Vegetable Couscous with Chick-Peas.

Commercially made European- and American-style noodles are made from durum flour and must, by law, contain 5.5 percent egg solids. Medium and wide egg noodles, bow ties and so on are used as accompaniments for stews and cooked meat, especially when the latter is served with gravy. Fine egg noodles are often added to soup. Many Asian-style noodles, usually made without egg, are also on the market today. Those made of wheat include the Chinese lo mein and the Japanese udon.

Chicken Nuggets with Sweet-and-Sour Dipping Sauce

4 SERVINGS

¼ *cup plus 2 tablespoons orange juice*
¼ *cup honey*
2 *teaspoons Asian sesame oil*
1 *pound skinless, boneless chicken breasts, cut into 1-inch chunks*
¼ *cup rice wine vinegar*
¼ *cup reduced-sodium soy sauce*
2 *teaspoons grated fresh ginger*
1 *cup wheat germ*
⅓ *cup sesame seeds, preferably unhulled*
¼ *teaspoon salt*
¼ *teaspoon pepper*
¼ *teaspoon garlic powder*

1. Lightly coat a 9-inch square baking pan with vegetable cooking spray. In a medium bowl, combine ¼ cup orange juice, 2 tablespoons honey and the sesame oil. Whisk to blend well. Add the chicken pieces and turn to coat. Cover the bowl with plastic wrap and marinate in the refrigerator for 1 hour.

2. In a small bowl, combine 2 tablespoons orange juice, the remaining 2 tablespoons honey, the vinegar, soy sauce and ginger. Whisk to blend. Set the sweet-and-sour dipping sauce aside.

3. In a shallow dish or pie plate, combine the wheat germ, sesame seeds, salt, pepper and garlic powder. Remove the chicken from the marinade. Add them to the wheat germ mixture and toss to coat. Place them in the prepared pan. Preheat the oven to 400 degrees.

4. Bake the chicken nuggets until white throughout but still juicy, 18 to 20 minutes, turning the pieces after 10 minutes. Raise the temperature to broil and broil until browned and crisp, about 5 minutes. Serve with the sweet-and-sour dipping sauce.

Calories: 409	Protein: 38 gm	Total Fat: 13 gm
Saturated Fat: 2 gm	Cholesterol: 66 mg	Carbohydrates: 39 gm
Sodium: 816 mg	Dietary Fiber: 4 gm	

A SUPER SOURCE OF:

Phosphorus	65%
Iron	31%
Thiamin	43%
Riboflavin	22%
Niacin	78%
Vitamin C	21%
Zinc	44%

0%   U.S. Recommended Daily Allowance   100%

Roasted Eggplant and Bulgur

4 SERVINGS

1 medium eggplant, halved lengthwise
1 tablespoon olive oil
1 large onion, chopped
1 large garlic clove, minced
¾ cup bulgur
1½ cups chicken stock or canned low-sodium broth
¾ teaspoon salt
¼ teaspoon pepper
¼ cup chopped parsley

1. Preheat the broiler. Lightly coat a small baking dish with vegetable cooking spray. Place the eggplant halves, cut side down, in the baking dish. Broil about 4 inches from the heat until the skin is charred and the pulp is soft, about 20 minutes. Remove the eggplant from the oven. Let it stand 5 minutes, until slightly cooled. Reduce the oven temperature to 400 degrees.

2. With a large spoon, scoop the eggplant from the skin, leaving a ¼-inch shell. Coarsely chop the eggplant. Set the eggplant shells aside.

3. In a large skillet, heat the olive oil over medium heat. Add the onion and garlic and cook until soft but not brown, 3 to 5 minutes. Add the chopped eggplant and cook, stirring, 2 minutes longer.

4. Stir in the bulgur. Reduce the heat to medium-low. Add the stock and simmer, covered, until the liquid is absorbed, about 10 minutes. Add the salt, pepper and parsley.

5. Spoon the eggplant mixture into the hollowed-out eggplant shells. Put back in the baking dish and bake until heated through and crispy on top, 5 to 7 minutes. Cut each half into 2 portions and serve warm.

Calories: 181	Protein: 6 gm	Total Fat: 4 gm
Saturated Fat: 1 gm	Cholesterol: 0 mg	Carbohydrates: 32 gm
Sodium: 444 mg	Dietary Fiber: 8 gm	

Bulgur is an excellent source of folic acid. A 1-ounce portion (about 3½ tablespoons uncooked) provides nearly a third of the adult Recommended Daily Allowance of this vitamin essential to basic cellular activities.

Mediterranean Vegetable Bulgur Salad

The amino acids in bulgur and chick-peas combine to form complete protein, which helps make this salad nourishing and filling. After tossing, the mixture can be heaped on a platter lined with romaine lettuce for an attractive presentation. 6 SERVINGS

½ cup medium bulgur
3 radishes, coarsely chopped
½ cup canned chick-peas (garbanzo beans), rinsed and drained
2 tablespoons chopped pitted black olives
4 scallions, chopped
1 carrot, chopped
1 green bell pepper, chopped
1 tomato, seeded and cut into ½-inch dice
½ cup chopped parsley
¼ cup chopped fresh mint
1 cup nonfat plain yogurt
1 garlic clove, minced
¼ cup olive oil, preferably extra virgin
3 tablespoons fresh lemon juice
1 teaspoon cumin
½ teaspoon salt
¼ teaspoon pepper

1. In a medium saucepan, combine the bulgur with 1 cup water. Bring to a boil. Reduce the heat to a simmer, cover and cook for 10 minutes, or until the liquid is absorbed. Set aside to cool.

2. In a large bowl, combine the radishes, chick-peas, olives, scallions, carrot, green pepper, tomato, parsley and mint.

3. Prepare a dressing by mixing the yogurt, garlic, olive oil, lemon juice, cumin, salt and pepper in a small bowl or by shaking the ingredients together in a jar with a tight-fitting lid. Pour the dressing over the salad and toss until evenly combined.

Calories: 182	Protein: 5 gm	Total Fat: 10 gm
Saturated Fat: 1 gm	Cholesterol: 1 mg	Carbohydrates: 19 gm
Sodium: 274 mg	Dietary Fiber: 4 gm	

A SUPER SOURCE OF:

Vitamin A	━━━━━━━━━━━━━━━━	91%
Vitamin C	━━━━━━━━━━ 58%	

0%   U.S. Recommended Daily Allowance   100%

*T*abbouleh

Consider this recipe as a jumping off point for endless improvisation. Tiny cooked shrimp, a bit of crumbled feta cheese, strips of sweet red bell pepper or a few anchovies, for example, would all be flavorful additions. 9 SERVINGS

2 cups bulgur
½ cup chopped fresh parsley
¼ cup chopped fresh mint
4 scallions, chopped
2 medium tomatoes, seeded and chopped into ¼-inch dice
1 cucumber, peeled and chopped into ¼-inch dice
3 tablespoons olive oil, preferably extra virgin
3 tablespoons fresh lemon juice
1 teaspoon salt
¼ teaspoon pepper
½ teaspoon cumin

1. In a large bowl, soak the bulgur in 4 cups boiling water for 30 minutes. Drain in a fine-mesh sieve, pressing out as much water as possible. Place in a large salad bowl.

2. Add the parsley, mint, scallions, tomatoes and cucumber. Mix well to blend.

3. In a small bowl, combine the olive oil, lemon juice, salt, pepper and cumin. Whisk until combined. Pour over the bulgur mixture and toss to mix evenly.

Calories: 160	Protein: 4 gm	Total Fat: 5 gm
Saturated Fat: 1 gm	Cholesterol: 0 mg	Carbohydrates: 27 gm
Sodium: 255 mg	Dietary Fiber: 6 gm	

A SUPER SOURCE OF:
Vitamin C ━━━━━ 27%

0%   U.S. Recommended Daily Allowance   100%

A 1-ounce portion (about 3½ tablespoons uncooked) of bulgur provides 96 calories from 21 grams of carbohydrate, 3 grams of protein and less than 1 gram of fat.

Roast Chicken and Bulgur with Oregano Yogurt Dressing

5 SERVINGS

1 pound chicken breasts, skin removed
½ cup plus 1 tablespoon chopped parsley
2 garlic cloves, minced
1½ teaspoons oregano
⅛ teaspoon crushed hot pepper flakes
3 tablespoons fresh lemon juice
1 cup bulgur
2 cups water
1 large tomato, seeded and cut into ½-inch dice
1 cucumber, peeled, halved lengthwise, seeded and sliced
4 scallions, chopped
2 tablespoons chopped fresh mint
¼ cup olive oil, preferably extra virgin
½ teaspoon salt
¼ teaspoon pepper
1 cup nonfat plain yogurt

1. Preheat the oven to 375 degrees. Place the chicken in an 8-inch square baking pan. In a small bowl, combine 1 tablespoon parsley, half the garlic, 1 teaspoon oregano, the hot pepper flakes and 1 tablespoon lemon juice. Brush over the chicken breasts.

2. Bake the chicken until tender, about 45 minutes. Cool and remove the chicken from the bones. Cut into 1-inch chunks.

3. In a medium saucepan, place the bulgur and water. Bring to a boil. Reduce the heat and simmer, covered, for 10 minutes, or until the liquid is absorbed.

4. Place the bulgur in a large bowl. Add the baked chicken, tomato, cucumber, scallions, ½ cup parsley, mint, olive oil, 2 tablespoons lemon juice, salt and pepper. Mix well.

5. In a small bowl, combine the yogurt, remaining garlic and ½ teaspoon oregano. Pour over the salad and toss well to combine.

Calories: 305	Protein: 21 gm	Total Fat: 13 gm
Saturated Fat: 2 gm	Cholesterol: 35 mg	Carbohydrates: 30 gm
Sodium: 305 mg	Dietary Fiber: 6 gm	

A SUPER SOURCE OF:

Phosphorus	━━━━━━━ 30%
Vitamin A	━━━━━━ 28%
Niacin	━━━━━━━━ 42%
Vitamin C	━━━━━━━━ 46%

0%   U.S. Recommended Daily Allowance   100%

Vegetable Couscous with Chick-Peas

Chick-peas, also called garbanzo beans and ceci, add fiber and protein to this harvest-inspired main course. Look for chick-peas in the Spanish and Italian sections of your supermarket. 6 SERVINGS

4 cups water
2 cups quick-cooking couscous
2 tablespoons olive oil, preferably extra virgin
1 teaspoon paprika
½ teaspoon cumin
½ teaspoon salt
¼ teaspoon cayenne pepper
1 medium onion, chopped
2 garlic cloves, minced
½ medium green bell pepper, chopped
½ medium red bell pepper, chopped
1 zucchini, chopped into ¼-inch dice
1 medium tomato, seeded and chopped into ¼-inch dice
1 cup canned chick-peas, rinsed and drained

1. In a medium saucepan, heat the water to boiling over high heat. Stir in the couscous. Reduce the heat to a simmer and cook, covered, until the couscous is tender, about 5 minutes. Fluff the grains of couscous with a fork and let cool.

2. In a large skillet, heat the oil over medium-high heat. Add the paprika, cumin, salt and cayenne pepper and cook for 1 minute, stirring frequently. Add the onion, garlic and green and red bell peppers. Cook, stirring occasionally, until softened, 3 to 5 minutes.

3. Stir in the zucchini and tomato. Cook until slightly softened, about 3 minutes. Add the chick-peas. Cook 2 minutes longer, until heated through. Mound the couscous on a large platter. Top with the cooked vegetables.

Calories: 323	Protein: 10 gm	Total Fat: 6 gm
Saturated Fat: 1 gm	Cholesterol: 0 mg	Carbohydrates: 56 gm
Sodium: 246 mg	Dietary Fiber: not available	

A SUPER SOURCE OF:

Vitamin A ━━━━━ 20%
Vitamin C ━━━━━━━━━ 46%

0%   U.S. Recommended Daily Allowance   100%

Gazpacho-Couscous Salad

6 SERVINGS

2 cups water
1½ cups quick-cooking couscous
½ cup no-salt-added vegetable juice
2 tablespoons safflower oil
2 tablespoons red wine vinegar
1 garlic clove, minced
1 tablespoon prepared white horseradish
¼ cup chopped fresh cilantro or parsley
½ teaspoon salt
¼ teaspoon pepper
2 medium tomatoes, cut into thin wedges
1 cucumber, peeled and chopped into ¼-inch dice
4 scallions, chopped
½ green bell pepper, chopped
½ red bell pepper, chopped
2 radishes, thinly sliced
1 celery stalk, sliced

1. In a medium saucepan, heat the water to boiling over high heat. Stir in the couscous. Reduce the heat to a simmer, cover and cook until the water is absorbed, about 5 minutes. Fluff the grains of couscous with a fork. Transfer to a large bowl and let cool.

2. Prepare a dressing by mixing the vegetable juice, oil, vinegar, garlic, horseradish, cilantro, salt and pepper in a small bowl or by shaking the ingredients together in a jar with a tight-fitting lid.

3. Add the tomatoes, cucumber, scallions, green and red bell peppers, radishes and celery to the couscous. Pour the dressing over the salad and toss until evenly combined.

Calories: 241	Protein: 7 gm	Total Fat: 5 gm
Saturated Fat: 0 gm	Cholesterol: 0 mg	Carbohydrates: 42 gm
Sodium: 208 mg	Dietary Fiber: not available	

A SUPER SOURCE OF:

Vitamin A ━━━━━━━ 36%
Vitamin C ━━━━━━━━━━━━━━━━ 69%

0%   U.S. Recommended Daily Allowance   100%

Couscous with Lamb and Slivered Almonds

4 SERVINGS

¼ cup slivered almonds
1 pound boneless lamb, cut into 1-inch cubes
¼ cup dry red wine
¼ cup red wine vinegar
1 tablespoon olive oil, preferably extra virgin
1 garlic clove, minced
½ teaspoon oregano
½ teaspoon rosemary
½ teaspoon salt
¼ teaspoon pepper
2 cups beef stock or canned low-sodium broth
1⅓ cups quick-cooking couscous

1. Preheat the oven to 325 degrees. Place the almonds on a small baking sheet. Bake, shaking the pan once or twice, until the nuts are golden and lightly toasted, 6 to 8 minutes. Remove from the pan and let cool completely.

2. Place the lamb in a shallow baking dish large enough to hold the meat in a single layer. In a small bowl, whisk together the wine, vinegar, oil, garlic, oregano, rosemary, salt and pepper. Pour over the lamb and turn the meat to coat. Marinate at room temperature for 1 hour or in the refrigerator for up to 8 hours. Remove the meat from the dish; reserve the marinade.

3. Preheat the broiler. Broil the lamb about 4 inches from the heat, turning and basting frequently with the reserved marinade, until pink and tender, 4 to 6 minutes.

4. Meanwhile, in a medium saucepan, heat the stock over high heat to boiling. Stir in the couscous. Reduce the heat to a simmer, cover and cook until the stock is absorbed, about 5 minutes. Mound the couscous on a large platter. Top with the lamb. Sprinkle on the toasted almonds.

Calories: 476	Protein: 33 gm	Total Fat: 15 gm
Saturated Fat: 3 gm	Cholesterol: 74 mg	Carbohydrates: 52 gm
Sodium: 358 mg	Dietary Fiber: not available	

A SUPER SOURCE OF:

Phosphorus	▬▬▬▬▬▬ 37%
Vitamin B12	▬▬▬▬▬▬▬▬ 52%
Niacin	▬▬▬▬▬▬▬ 46%
Zinc	▬▬▬▬▬▬ 36%

0%   U.S. Recommended Daily Allowance   100%

Curried Cracked Wheat and Shrimp Salad

Middle Eastern and Indian traditions combine in this culinary collaboration of marinated vegetables, curried bulgur, cooked shrimp and roasted peppers. 5 SERVINGS

2 carrots, sliced
¼ cup olive oil, preferably extra virgin
2 tablespoons white wine vinegar
2 scallions, chopped
1 tablespoon chopped pimiento
1 garlic clove, minced
½ teaspoon salt
¼ teaspoon pepper
1 tablespoon unsalted butter
1 small onion, chopped
1 teaspoon curry powder
2 teaspoons tomato paste
¾ cup medium bulgur
1½ cups chicken stock or canned low-sodium broth
2 medium green bell peppers, chopped
1 pound shrimp, cooked, shelled and deveined
¼ cup chopped parsley
2 tablespoons chopped pitted green olives

1. In a small saucepan of boiling water, cook the carrots until crisp-tender, 5 to 6 minutes. Drain.

2. In a small bowl, whisk together the oil, vinegar, scallions, pimiento, garlic, salt and pepper. Add the carrots and toss to coat. Marinate the carrots, tossing occasionally, for 1 hour.

3. In a medium skillet, melt the butter over medium heat. Add the onion and cook until soft but not brown, about 5 minutes. Add the curry powder and cook, stirring, for 1 minute. Stir in the tomato paste, bulgur and stock.

4. Bring to a boil, stirring. Reduce the heat to medium-low and simmer, covered, for 10 minutes, or until the liquid is absorbed. Transfer to a large bowl and let cool.

5. Preheat the broiler. Place the peppers on a small broiler pan. Broil, turning, until the peppers are charred and blistered all over. Remove them from the pan and place in a paper bag. Let the peppers steam in the bag until they are cool enough to handle, about 10 minutes. Remove the skin, seeds and ribs.

6. Chop the peppers and add them to the bulgur mixture. Add the carrots with their marinade, the shrimp, parsley and olives. Stir to combine. Serve the salad warm or at room temperature.

Calories: 310   Protein: 19 gm   Total Fat: 16 gm
Saturated Fat: 3 gm   Cholesterol: 118 mg   Carbohydrates: 24 gm
Sodium: 460 mg   Dietary Fiber: 6 gm

A SUPER SOURCE OF:

Phosphorus   ━━━━━━ 25%
Iron   ━━━━━ 20%
Vitamin A   ━━━━━━━━━━━━━━━━━━━━━━━━━━━━━━━━━ 100%
Niacin   ━━━━━ 20%
Vitamin C   ━━━━━━━━━━━━━━━━━━━━━━━━━━ 83%

0%   U.S. Recommended Daily Allowance   100%

*T*omatoes Stuffed with Minted Couscous

Traditionally steamed in a special double boiler called a *couscousière*, here readily available quick-cooking couscous is prepared quickly in an ordinary covered saucepan. 6 SERVINGS

6 medium tomatoes
2 cups water
1½ cups quick-cooking couscous
½ teaspoon salt
¼ teaspoon pepper
1 tablespoon olive oil
1 medium carrot, chopped
1 medium onion, chopped
2 tablespoons pine nuts
¼ cup chopped fresh mint

1. With a sharp knife, cut a thin slice from the top of each tomato. Remove the seeds and scoop out and reserve the pulp.

2. In a medium saucepan, heat the water over high heat to boiling. Stir in the couscous. Add the salt and pepper. Reduce the heat to a simmer, cover and cook, until the water is absorbed, about 5 minutes. Place the couscous in a large bowl and let cool for 15 minutes.

3. In a medium skillet, heat the oil over medium-high heat. Add the carrot and cook until crisp-tender, about 5 minutes. Add the onion and cook until soft but not brown, about 5 minutes. Stir in the reserved tomato pulp and cook until the liquid from the tomatoes has evaporated, 3 to 4 minutes. Place the vegetables in a bowl and let cool slightly, about 10 minutes.

4. Add the vegetables to the couscous and mix to blend. Stir in the pine nuts and mint. Fill the hollowed-out tomatoes with the couscous mixture. Serve warm or at room temperature.

Calories: 242	Protein: 8 gm	Total Fat: 4 gm
Saturated Fat: 1 gm	Cholesterol: 0 mg	Carbohydrates: 44 gm
Sodium: 201 mg	Dietary Fiber: not available	

A SUPER SOURCE OF:

Vitamin A	━━━━━━━━━━━━━━━━	97%
Vitamin C	━━━━━━━━	41%

0%   U.S. Recommended Daily Allowance   100%

*P*umpkin Pie Muffins

Pumpkin adds moistness and a bonus of fiber to these autumnal muffins. Placed in a basket with Very Corny Muffins (p. 46), they'd provide a flavorful and appropriate addition to any Thanksgiving feast. MAKES 12 MUFFINS

1 cup whole wheat flour
½ cup all-purpose flour
⅓ cup packed brown sugar
2 teaspoons baking powder
½ teaspoon baking soda
1 teaspoon cinnamon
¼ teaspoon ginger
¼ teaspoon nutmeg
¼ teaspoon salt
¼ cup raisins
¾ cup canned solid pack pumpkin
¼ cup safflower oil
¼ cup nonfat plain yogurt
1 egg

1. Preheat the oven to 375 degrees. Line a 12-count muffin tin with paper baking cups.
2. In a large bowl, combine the whole wheat flour, all-purpose flour, brown sugar, baking powder, baking soda, cinnamon, ginger, nutmeg, salt and raisins.
3. In a medium bowl, place the pumpkin, oil, yogurt and egg. Whisk until well blended. Add all at once to the dry ingredients. Stir only until moistened; the batter should be slightly lumpy.
4. Spoon the batter evenly into the prepared pan. Bake 20 to 25 minutes, or until the muffins are golden and springy to the touch. Remove the muffins from the pan and let cool on a wire rack.

Calories per muffin: 140	Protein: 3 gm	Total Fat: 5 gm
Saturated Fat: 1 gm	Cholesterol: 18 mg	Carbohydrates: 21 gm
Sodium: 163 mg	Dietary Fiber: 2 gm	

A SUPER SOURCE OF:
Vitamin A ━━━━━━━━━━━━━ 68%

0%   U.S. Recommended Daily Allowance   100%

A 1-ounce portion (about ¼ cup) of wheat germ provides 100 calories from 12 grams of carbohydrate, 9 grams of protein and 3 grams of fat. The carbohydrates include 3.3 grams of dietary fiber.

*W*hole Wheat Applesauce Waffles

Try these spicy waffles with a dollop of plain low-fat yogurt and a spoonful of dark brown sugar. In a matter of minutes, the sugar magically melts to a syrupy glaze. 4 SERVINGS

1¼ cups all-purpose flour
½ cup whole wheat flour
1 tablespoon packed brown sugar
2 teaspoons baking powder
½ teaspoon baking soda
½ teaspoon cinnamon
1 egg
1 cup skim milk
½ cup unsweetened applesauce
2 tablespoons safflower oil

1. Preheat and lightly coat a waffle iron with vegetable cooking spray.
2. In a medium bowl, place the all-purpose flour, whole wheat flour, brown sugar, baking powder, baking soda and cinnamon.
3. In a small bowl, thoroughly combine the egg, milk, applesauce and oil. Add the liquid ingredients to the dry ingredients and stir until just moistened; the batter should be slightly lumpy.
4. Pour about ⅓ cup of the batter onto the prepared waffle iron and cook 4 to 5 minutes, or until golden brown and crisp. Repeat with the remaining batter. Serve the waffles hot.

Calories: 323	Protein: 10 gm	Total Fat: 9 gm
Saturated Fat: 1 gm	Cholesterol: 54 mg	Carbohydrates: 51 gm
Sodium: 366 mg	Dietary Fiber: 3 gm	

A SUPER SOURCE OF:

Calcium	━━━━━	21%
Phosphorus	━━━━━	21%
Thiamin	━━━━━	25%
Riboflavin	━━━━━	21%

0%   U.S. Recommended Daily Allowance   100%

Whole wheat flour contains a spoilable oil that can cause a storage problem, especially in hot weather. An unopened bag usually can be stored in a cool place for up to 3 months. After opening, put the flour into an airtight container and store in the refrigerator or freezer for up to 3 months more.

Very Light Whole Wheat Bread

This loaf, which also includes rolled oats, is a good introduction to whole wheat breads. Even people who think they won't like it are pleasantly surprised at how good it tastes. It's light in texture but hearty in flavor. MAKES 1 LOAF, 14 SLICES

1 cup warm water (105 to 115 degrees)
2 teaspoons honey
1 envelope active dry yeast
1²/₃ cups bread flour
²/₃ cup whole wheat flour
²/₃ cup regular or quick-cooking oats
1 teaspoon salt
Cornmeal
1 egg white, beaten

1. In a small bowl, place the water and honey. Stir in the yeast. Let stand until foamy, about 5 minutes.

2. In a food processor fitted with the metal blade, place 1⅓ cups of the bread flour, the whole wheat flour, oats and salt. With the machine on, add the yeast mixture through the feed tube. When it forms a ball, process 45 seconds longer, until the dough is smooth and elastic. If the dough is too wet and doesn't form a ball, add the remaining ⅓ cup bread flour 1 tablespoon at a time. If using a hand-held electric mixer, combine ⅓ cup bread flour, the whole wheat flour, the oats and salt in a large bowl. Add the yeast mixture and mix at medium speed for 2 minutes. Decrease the speed to low and mix 2 minutes. Remove the beaters and stir in enough remaining bread flour, ⅓ cup at a time, to form a dough that pulls away from the sides of the bowl.

3. Turn the dough out onto a lightly floured surface and knead by hand 8 to 10 minutes, or until the dough is smooth and elastic. If prepared with the processor, the dough has already been kneaded.

4. Lightly spray a large bowl with vegetable cooking spray. Place the dough in the bowl and turn to coat evenly. Cover the dough and let rise in a warm draft-free area for 1 hour, or until it is doubled in size.

5. On a lightly floured surface, roll out the dough into a 10 × 15−inch rectangle. Beginning with a short end, roll up the dough. Pinch the ends and seam together to seal. Lightly coat a 9 × 5 × 3−inch loaf pan with vegetable cooking spray and dust with cornmeal. Place the dough, seam side down, in the prepared pan. Cover and let rise 45 minutes, or until it is almost doubled in size. Preheat the oven to 375 degrees.

6. Brush the top of the dough with the egg white. Bake 35 minutes, or until the crust is golden and sounds hollow when tapped. Cool on a wire rack.

Calories per slice: 102	Protein: 4 gm	Total Fat: 1 gm
Saturated Fat: 0 gm	Cholesterol: 0 mg	Carbohydrates: 20 gm
Sodium: 162 mg	Dietary Fiber: 1 gm	

*W*hole Wheat Pita

Baking your own pitas is an experience you don't want to miss. Watching them puff up in the oven, and after they cool, opening them to reveal that special pocket, can astonish even the most experienced baker. MAKES 18 PITA BREADS

2 cups warm water (105 to 115 degrees)
2 teaspoons sugar
2 envelopes active dry yeast
3 to 3½ cups bread flour
2 cups whole wheat flour
1 teaspoon salt

1. In a large mixing bowl, combine the warm water and sugar. Stir in the yeast. Let it stand until foamy, about 5 minutes.

2. Add 2 cups of the bread flour, all of the whole wheat flour and the salt to the yeast mixture. Using a hand-held electric mixer, beat at medium speed for 2 minutes. Decrease the speed to low and mix 2 minutes longer. Remove the beaters and stir in enough remaining bread flour, ¼ cup at a time, to form a dough that pulls away from the sides of the bowl.

3. Turn the dough out onto a lightly floured surface and knead by hand for 8 to 10 minutes, or until the dough is smooth and elastic.

4. Lightly spray a large bowl with vegetable cooking spray. Place the dough in a bowl and turn to coat evenly. Cover the dough and let rise in a warm draft-free area for 1 hour, or until it has doubled in size.

5. Divide the risen dough into 18 pieces. Shape each piece into a ball. Cover balls with plastic wrap to prevent them from drying out.

6. Roll out each ball into a 6-inch circle, rolling from the center and rotating a quarter turn after each roll. Place each rolled circle on a lightly floured board. Cover the dough and let rise in a draft-free area for 30 minutes. They will not fully double in size.

7. Place an ungreased cookie sheet in the oven and preheat the oven to 500 degrees for 10 minutes. After 10 minutes, bake 4 of the pita rounds on the lowest oven rack for about 5 minutes, or until puffed and lightly colored. Remove them from the oven and wrap in dry towels for about 3 minutes, or until they have cooled slightly. Place an empty cookie sheet in the oven and heat for 10 minutes. Repeat the baking and cooling process with each batch until all the dough is baked.

Calories per pita: 138	Protein: 5 gm	Total Fat: 1 gm
Saturated Fat: 0 gm	Cholesterol: 0 mg	Carbohydrates: 28 gm
Sodium: 124 mg	Dietary Fiber: 2 gm	

The bran in whole wheat flour reduces its gluten strength so that bread baked with a high percentage of whole wheat flour does not rise as much as bread baked with white flour alone.

Whole Wheat Pita Crisps

You can find packaged pita crisps at many markets, but they're easy to make at home. Offered here are sweet and savory versions.

Sweet Pita Crisps

MAKES 24 WEDGES

2 whole wheat pita breads, about 6 inches in diameter (see p. 26)
2 tablespoons unsalted butter, melted
1½ teaspoons cinnamon
½ teaspoon nutmeg
¼ teaspoon mace

1. Preheat the oven to 350 degrees. Lightly coat a cookie sheet with vegetable cooking spray. Split the pita breads into 2 thin rounds each.

2. In a small bowl, combine the butter, cinnamon, nutmeg and mace. Brush lightly over the pita halves.

3. Cut each pita half into 6 wedges. Place on prepared pan. Bake until crisp, about 10 minutes. Cool on a wire rack.

Calories per wedge: 23	Protein: 1 gm	Total Fat: 1 gm
Saturated Fat: 1 gm	Cholesterol: 3 mg	Carbohydrates: 3 gm
Sodium: 30 mg	Dietary Fiber: 0 gm	

Savory Pita Crisps

MAKES 24 WEDGES

2 whole wheat pita breads, about 6 inches in diameter (see p. 26)
2 tablespoons olive oil
1 garlic clove, minced
1 tablespoon grated Parmesan cheese
1 teaspoon oregano

1. Preheat the oven to 350 degrees. Lightly coat a cookie sheet with vegetable cooking spray. Split the pita breads into 2 thin rounds each.

2. In a small bowl, combine the oil, garlic, cheese and oregano. Brush lightly over the pita halves.

3. Cut each pita half into 6 wedges. Place on prepared pan. Bake until crisp on top, about 10 minutes. Cool on a wire rack.

Calories: 25 per wedge	Protein: 1 gm	Total Fat: 1 gm
Saturated Fat: 0 gm	Cholesterol: 0 mg	Sodium: 34 mg
Dietary Fiber: 0 gm		

Stuffed Whole Wheat Pitas

Mini pitas are just the right size for little hands. Filled with turkey, lettuce and tomato and packed into a lunch bag, they're perfect for midday munching. 2 SERVINGS

1 tablespoon nonfat plain yogurt
1 tablespoon reduced-calorie, no-cholesterol mayonnaise
4 mini whole wheat pita breads, about 3½ inches in
  diameter, partially opened
¼ pound turkey breast, cut into strips
½ cup shredded lettuce
1 medium tomato, seeded and cut into ½-inch dice

1. In a small bowl, combine the yogurt and mayonnaise. With a pastry brush, lightly brush the inside of the pitas with the mixture.
2. Fill the pitas with the turkey, lettuce and tomato. Allow 2 per serving.

Calories: 297	Protein: 27 gm	Total Fat: 5 gm
Saturated Fat: 1 gm	Cholesterol: 39 mg	Carbohydrates: 39 gm
Sodium: 155 mg	Dietary Fiber: 5 gm	

A SUPER SOURCE OF:
Niacin ━━━━━━ 23%

└─   ─┘
0%   U.S. Recommended Daily Allowance   100%

Health-food and specialty stores often sell what's called "gluten flour." This is flour that has been washed with water to remove some of the starch, then dried and remilled. It can be made into high-protein bread or mixed with low-gluten flours to give bread dough a better rise, a useful approach when you're adding whole grain flours or bran to the mix.

Super Duper Tuna Pasta Salad

This salad tastes even better the second day, if there is any left over. Medium shells can be used in place of the elbows. 4 SERVINGS

2 cups whole wheat elbow macaroni
2 cans (7 ounces each) water-packed white tuna, drained and flaked
1 hard-cooked egg, finely diced
1 celery stalk, chopped
½ carrot, grated
½ cup nonfat plain yogurt
¼ cup reduced-calorie, no-cholesterol mayonnaise
3 tablespoons dehydrated minced onions
1 tablespoon Dijon mustard
¼ teaspoon salt
¼ teaspoon pepper

1. In a large saucepan of boiling water, cook the macaroni until tender, about 6 to 8 minutes. Drain, rinse under cold water and drain well.

2. In a large bowl, combine the macaroni, tuna, egg, celery and carrot.

3. In a small bowl, prepare a dressing by whisking together the yogurt, mayonnaise, minced onions, mustard, salt and pepper. Spoon the dressing over the salad and toss until evenly combined.

Calories: 461	Protein: 36	Total Fat: 16 gm
Saturated Fat: 3 gm	Cholesterol: 101 mg	Carbohydrates: 46 gm
Sodium: 748 mg	Dietary Fiber: 7 gm	

A SUPER SOURCE OF:

Phosphorus	22%
Vitamin A	53%
Niacin	41%

0%   U.S. Recommended Daily Allowance   100%

When cooking pasta, add the product a bit at a time so the water maintains a rolling boil. When all has been added to the pot, begin timing. Leave pot uncovered and, to ensure even cooking, stir frequently.

Salmon, Green Bean and Macaroni Salad

This bright and beautiful salad tastes as good as it looks. Red salmon is the prettiest and most flavorful, but pink salmon can be used with satisfactory results. 4 SERVINGS

1 cup whole wheat elbow macaroni
1 large can (15½ ounces) red Sockeye salmon, drained and broken into chunks
½ pound fresh green beans, cut into 1-inch pieces, cooked and drained
1 small purple onion, chopped
½ cup part-skim ricotta cheese
3 tablespoons nonfat plain yogurt
2 tablespoons fresh lemon juice
1 tablespoon olive oil
1 tablespoon prepared white horseradish
2 tablespoons chopped fresh dill
½ teaspoon salt
¼ teaspoon white pepper

1. In a medium saucepan of boiling water, cook the macaroni until tender, 6 to 8 minutes. Drain, rinse under cold water and drain well.

2. In a large salad bowl, place the macaroni, salmon, green beans and onion.

3. In a blender or food processor, combine the ricotta cheese, yogurt, lemon juice, olive oil, horseradish, dill, salt and white pepper. Blend until smooth. Pour the dressing over the salad and toss to coat.

Calories: 332	Protein: 28 gm	Total Fat: 13 gm
Saturated Fat: 3 gm	Cholesterol: 49 mg	Carbohydrates: 28 gm
Sodium: 810 mg	Dietary Fiber: 4 gm	

A SUPER SOURCE OF:

Calcium	36%
Phosphorus	46%
Niacin	34%
Vitamin C	23%

0%   U.S. Recommended Daily Allowance   100%

Pasta is best when cooked to the firm-tender al dente stage. After 4 minutes or so, start testing the pasta for doneness by fishing out a strand or piece, cooling it quickly with cold water, and biting into it. The pasta should be firm but tender through its thickness, with no hard center.

Greek Salad with Whole Wheat Elbows

Whole wheat macaroni adds a new twist to this familiar salad. Tossed rather than composed, it is a snap to prepare. 4 SERVINGS

1 cup whole wheat elbow macaroni
1 medium zucchini, thinly sliced
1 medium red onion, chopped
1 large tomato, seeded and cut into ½-inch dice
1 medium cucumber, peeled, seeded, sliced diagonally
2 tablespoons chopped pitted black olives, preferably
   Calamata
¼ cup crumbled feta cheese
¼ cup olive oil, preferably extra virgin
2 tablespoons fresh lemon juice
¼ cup chopped fresh parsley
2 tablespoons chopped fresh dill or 1 teaspoon dried
1 garlic clove, minced
½ teaspoon salt
¼ teaspoon pepper

1. In a medium saucepan of boiling water, cook the macaroni until tender, about 6 to 8 minutes. Drain and cool.

2. In a large salad bowl, combine the macaroni, zucchini, onion, tomato, cucumber, olives and cheese.

3. Prepare a dressing by mixing the oil, lemon juice, parsley, dill, garlic, salt and pepper in a small bowl or by shaking the ingredients together in a jar with a tight-fitting lid. Pour the dressing over the salad and toss until evenly combined.

Calories: 271	Protein: 7 gm	Total Fat: 16 gm
Saturated Fat: 3 gm	Cholesterol: 8 mg	Carbohydrates: 28 gm
Sodium: 417 mg	Dietary Fiber: 5 gm	

A SUPER SOURCE OF:
Vitamin C ━━━━━━━━━ 42%

0%   U.S. Recommended Daily Allowance   100%

A side dish of pasta (2 ounces uncooked) typically provides 210 calories from 41 to 42 grams of carbohydrate, 7 to 8 grams of protein and 1 gram of fat.

*P*asta Salad with Eggplant and Capers

A full-bodied salad with some of the favored Mediterranean ingredients—eggplant, garlic, olives, capers, basil and tomatoes.

5 SERVINGS

2 cups whole wheat elbow macaroni
1 tablespoon olive oil, preferably extra virgin
1 medium eggplant, peeled and cut into ½-inch dice
1 onion, chopped
1 red bell pepper, chopped
2 garlic cloves, minced
⅓ cup canned crushed tomatoes, with their juice
2 tablespoons chopped pitted olives
2 tablespoons chopped fresh basil
1 cup chicken stock or canned low-sodium broth
2 tablespoons capers
1 teaspoon oregano
½ teaspoon salt
¼ teaspoon pepper
¼ cup grated Parmesan cheese

1. In a large saucepan of boiling water, cook the macaroni until tender, about 6 to 8 minutes. Drain, rinse under cold water and drain well.

2. In a large skillet, heat the oil over medium heat. Add the eggplant, onion, pepper and garlic and cook until soft, 6 to 8 minutes.

3. Add the tomatoes, olives and basil. Pour in the stock. Cook, stirring occasionally, 20 minutes longer, until about half the liquid evaporates and the vegetables form a thick stew. Add the capers, oregano, salt and pepper. Transfer the mixture to a large bowl and let cool for 15 minutes.

4. Add the pasta to the bowl with the eggplant-tomato mixture. Sprinkle on the cheese. Toss to mix. Serve at room temperature.

Calories: 241	Protein: 10 gm	Total Fat: 6 gm
Saturated Fat: 1 gm	Cholesterol: 3 mg	Carbohydrates: 42 gm
Sodium: 456 mg	Dietary Fiber: 7 gm	

A SUPER SOURCE OF:

Vitamin A ▬▬▬ 22%
Thiamin ▬▬▬ 20%
Vitamin C ▬▬▬▬▬ 57%

0%   U.S. Recommended Daily Allowance   100%

Cooked Wheat Berries

Preparation consists of soaking and cooking the berries before using them. Then they're ready to shine in salads, entrees, soups and even desserts. MAKES 3 CUPS

1½ cups wheat berries, picked over
5 cups water

1. In a large saucepan, combine the wheat berries and water. Cover and soak overnight.
2. Heat the wheat berries in the soaking water to boiling over high heat. Reduce the heat to a simmer, cover and cook until the wheat berries are tender but still firm, about 55 minutes.
3. Drain and let cool. Use as needed according to individual recipes. Refrigerate any extra wheat berries in a covered container. They will keep for up to 1 week.

Calories: 147 per ½ cup	Protein: 6 gm	Total Fat: 1 gm
Saturated Fat: 0 gm	Cholesterol: 0 mg	Carbohydrates: 29 gm
Sodium: 4 mg	Dietary Fiber: 0 gm	

A 1-ounce portion (about 2½ tablespoons uncooked) of wheat berries provides 92 calories from 20 grams of carbohydrate, 3 grams of protein and less than 1 gram of fat. Wheat berries are also a good source of phosphorus and thiamin.

*Z*ucchini *Wheat Berry Bars*

These spicy squares are moist and tasty. Wheat berries are the surprise ingredient, adding an unusual and pleasing texture.

MAKES 16 SQUARES

1¼ cups all-purpose flour
½ cup cooked wheat berries (see p. 33)
2 teaspoons baking powder
½ teaspoon baking soda
2 teaspoons cinnamon
¼ teaspoon grated nutmeg
¼ teaspoon ground cloves
⅓ cup honey
1 cup buttermilk
¼ cup safflower oil
1 whole large egg
2 egg whites
1 cup grated zucchini
⅓ cup raisins

1. Preheat the oven to 375 degrees. Lightly coat an 8-inch square baking pan with vegetable cooking spray.

2. In a large bowl, combine the all-purpose flour, wheat berries, baking powder, baking soda, cinnamon, nutmeg and cloves.

3. In a medium bowl, combine the honey, buttermilk, oil, whole egg and egg whites. Whisk until well blended. Stir in the zucchini and raisins. Add the flour mixture to the liquid ingredients. Stir until just combined.

4. Spread the batter into the prepared pan. Bake 35 to 40 minutes, or until a toothpick inserted in the center comes out clean. Cool the cake in the pan on a wire rack. Cut into 2-inch squares.

Calories: 120	Protein: 3 gm	Total Fat: 4 gm
Saturated Fat: 0 gm	Cholesterol: 14 mg	Carbohydrates: 19 gm
Sodium: 107 mg	Dietary Fiber: 0 gm	

*W*heat Berry and Roasted Red Pepper Salad with Garlic Dressing

Try this hearty wheat berry salad. The peppers and garlic are wondrously sweet and flavorful. If you've never baked garlic cloves before, this recipe is a great way to begin. SERVES 4

2 red bell peppers
2 garlic cloves, unpeeled
¼ cup chicken stock or canned low-sodium broth
3 scallions, chopped
3 cups cooked wheat berries (see p. 33)
2 teaspoons Dijon mustard
3 tablespoons olive oil, preferably extra virgin
2 tablespoons red wine vinegar
¼ cup chopped fresh parsley
½ teaspoon salt
¼ teaspoon pepper

1. Preheat the broiler. Place the peppers on a small broiler pan. Broil about 4 inches from the heat, turning, until the peppers are charred and blistered all over, about 10 minutes. Remove them from the pan and place in a paper bag. Let the peppers steam in the bag until they are cool enough to handle, about 10 minutes. Remove the skin, seeds and ribs. Chop the peppers and set aside.

2. Preheat the oven to 350 degrees. In a small baking dish, place the garlic cloves and the stock; turn the garlic to coat. Bake 30 to 35 minutes, until tender. Let cool. Peel and mash the garlic to a paste.

3. Place the peppers, scallions and wheat berries in a large bowl. Prepare a dressing by mixing the garlic, mustard, olive oil, vinegar, parsley, salt and pepper in a small bowl, or by shaking the ingredients together in a jar with a tight-fitting lid. Pour the dressing over the salad and toss until evenly combined.

Calories: 332	Protein: 10 gm	Total Fat: 13 gm
Saturated Fat: 2 gm	Cholesterol: 0 mg	Carbohydrates: 48 gm
Sodium: 361 mg	Dietary Fiber: 1 gm	

A SUPER SOURCE OF:

Iron	━━━━ 23%
Vitamin A	━━━━━━━━━ 57%
Niacin	━━━━ 24%
Vitamin C	━━━━━━━━━━━━━━━━━ 100%

0%   U.S. Recommended Daily Allowance   100%

COOKING WITH CORN

The next time you bite into an ear of corn that's speckled with pepper and dripping butter, consider that the vegetable you're eating is actually a grain. Corn is the one grain we can eat as a fresh vegetable; the large size of the kernels and their tenderness when young make that possible. As in other grains, corn kernels eventually turn rock hard, but young corn has a sugar-and-cream flavor and a succulence that's unique.

A sweet thought, when it comes to corn, is that anything that tastes so good can also be good for you. A medium-size ear—without butter—provides just 85 calories. That's a dietary bargain, considering the satisfaction one ear provides.

The variety of corn we eat fresh is properly called *sweet corn*. It's now available year-round, but usually is best July through October. In storage, sweet corn should be kept cool and moist, and this is something to have in mind when shopping. Displayed dry, at room temperature, sweet corn loses about half its sugar in a single day.

The husks enclosing the ears should be fresh and green and fit snugly. The silk should be golden, moist, and show no signs of decay. If possible, peel back the husks and examine the kernels. They should be tightly packed, pale and plump; spaces between the rows, a darkish color, and kernels that are dented all indicate excessive age.

Our Very Corny Muffins and Lamb, Corn and Vegetable Kebabs gain a special something from the addition of sweet corn, the "vegetable grain." Baby corn, which is eaten cob and all, takes center stage in Superb Succotash Salad with Baby Corn and Slim Steak Stir-Fry with Baby Corn and Snow Peas.

Unlike the proverbial apple pie, which was brought here by European colonists, corn is indigenous to the New World. As a dried grain, corn has been on American tables for as long as Americans have had tables. Cornmeal is the most common form, followed by grits, hominy, polenta (more coarsely ground Italian-style cornmeal) and the finely ground masa harina ("dough flour") used by our neighbors south of the border.

A look at packages will reveal that some cornmeals are "whole grain" and some are "degermed," that a few are "stone-ground" and that many have been "enriched."

▲ **Whole-grain cornmeal** is made from the entire grain and is cornmeal in its most nutritious form. It will keep longest if stored in a tightly closed container in the refrigerator.

▲ **Degermed meal** is made of corn kernels from which the oily germ (which can turn rancid), the growing part of the seed, has been removed. Degermed meal keeps longer in the cupboard than whole-grain meal, but is less nutritious.

▲ **Stone-ground meal** is ground slowly between huge old-fashioned millstones. Enthusiasts say the grain doesn't get as hot that way and keeps more of its natural goodness. No matter how it's processed, however, cornmeal today is often enriched with iron and the B vitamins niacin, thiamin and riboflavin.

Traditionally, white cornmeal has been favored in the South, yellow cornmeal in the North. For recipe purposes, the two are interchangeable.

Cornmeal adds wonderful flavor and a pleasingly gritty texture to all kinds of baked goods, as you'll find if you try some of our favorites, such as Cornmeal Waffles, Peppery Corn Sticks and Blueberry Corn Muffins. These recipes, you'll notice, include wheat flour to bind the dough. If pure cornmeal is baked into bread, the loaf is brittle and crumbly. Varying the percentage of wheat flour lets you determine how smooth and cakelike or gritty and crumbly a corn bread or muffin will be.

Grits are coarsely ground dried hominy, which is corn with the hull and germ removed, usually by soaking in a lye solution. Dried hominy is available whole and cracked; whole hominy is also available canned. The hominy favored in Dixie is made from white corn. Many Latin-Americans prefer yellow hominy, however, and that's the choice for our savory Chicken Pozole.

Whether you're cooking with sweet corn, or with one of these forms of dried corn, here is an international assortment of recipes to help you add more good grain to your family's daily diet.

* Plain popcorn is an especially low-calorie snack food—just 27 calories to 1 cup.

Sugar content and flavor in sweet corn depends somewhat on color. Yellow varieties are typically richer and more "corny," while white and the bicolored "butter and sugar" corns tend to be sweeter and milder.

Superb Succotash Salad with Baby Corn

This updated rendition of the American classic substitutes whole baby corn for corn kernels and turns the hot side dish into a room temperature salad. 4 SERVINGS

1 box (10 ounces) frozen baby lima beans
½ cup boiling water
1 can (15 ounces) baby corn, rinsed and drained, or 1
   package (10 ounces) frozen, thawed
1 medium green bell pepper, chopped
1 celery stalk, chopped
2 scallions, chopped
¼ cup safflower oil
3 tablespoons white wine vinegar
2 tablespoons chopped parsley
1 garlic clove, minced
½ teaspoon salt
¼ teaspoon pepper

1. In a medium saucepan, cook the lima beans in the boiling water over medium-high heat until crisp-tender, about 7 minutes. Drain and cool.

2. In a medium salad bowl, place the lima beans, baby corn, bell pepper, celery and scallions.

3. In a small bowl, prepare a dressing by whisking together the oil, vinegar, parsley, garlic, salt and pepper, or by shaking the ingredients together in a jar with a tight-fitting lid. Pour the dressing over the salad and toss until evenly combined.

Calories: 250	Protein: 8 gm	Total Fat: 14 gm
Saturated Fat: 1 gm	Cholesterol: 0 mg	Carbohydrates: 24 gm
Sodium: 330 mg	Dietary Fiber: 2 gm	

A SUPER SOURCE OF:

Vitamin C ━━━━━━━━━━━━━━━━ 67%

0%   U.S. Recommended Daily Allowance   100%

Some authorities say corn should be cooked in unsalted water; others suggest adding salt to the cooking water once the ears are half cooked. Either way, the aim is to preserve tenderness.

*V*elvet Corn and Crab Soup

A Hong Kong specialty sure to become a family favorite, this soup, loaded with chunks of crabmeat, has fabulous flavor.

6 SERVINGS

1 tablespoon Asian sesame oil
1 teaspoon grated fresh ginger
1 garlic clove, minced
4 cups chicken stock or canned low-sodium broth
1 can (14 ounces) reduced-sodium creamed corn
1 cup cooked flaked crabmeat pieces
1 brick (4 ounces) firm tofu, cut into ½-inch cubes
2 teaspoons cornstarch
2 tablespoons cold water
2 scallions, chopped

1. In a medium saucepan, heat the sesame oil over low heat. Add the ginger and garlic and cook until just golden, about 2 minutes.

2. Immediately add the chicken stock, raise the heat to medium-high and bring to a boil. Add the creamed corn, crabmeat and tofu. Reduce the heat to low and simmer 5 minutes.

3. In a small bowl, dissolve the cornstarch in the water. Stir into the hot soup and bring to a boil. Cook until slightly thickened, 1 to 2 minutes. Ladle the soup into bowls and garnish with the chopped scallions.

Calories: 147	Protein: 11 gm	Total Fat: 6 gm
Saturated Fat: 1 gm	Cholesterol: 26 mg	Carbohydrates: 15 gm
Sodium: 113 mg	Dietary Fiber: 1 gm	

A SUPER SOURCE OF:
Vitamin B12 ———————— 31%

0%   U.S. Recommended Daily Allowance   100%

Slim Steak Stir-Fry with Baby Corn and Snow Peas

This is a double-duty dish—great for the family and super for entertaining! 6 SERVINGS

2½ cups water
1 cup brown rice
½ teaspoon salt
2 tablespoons low-sodium soy sauce
¼ cup rice vinegar
1 teaspoon minced fresh ginger
¼ cup orange juice
1 teaspoon grated orange zest
¼ teaspoon ground pepper
1 pound flank steak
1 tablespoon safflower oil
1 medium green bell pepper, chopped
1 medium red bell pepper, chopped
3 scallions, chopped
1 garlic clove, minced
1 package (10 ounces) frozen baby corn, thawed, or 1 can
  (15 ounces) baby corn, drained
½ cup snow peas, strings removed

1. In a medium saucepan, heat the water over high heat to boiling. Add the brown rice and salt. Reduce the heat to a simmer, cover and cook until the rice is tender, about 45 minutes. Rinse the rice under cold water and drain well.

2. In a small bowl, combine the soy sauce, vinegar, ginger, orange juice, orange zest and pepper.

3. Slice the flank steak diagonally across the grain into thin strips. (This is easier if the meat is placed in the freezer for 30 minutes.) Place the steak and the soy mixture in a shallow baking dish. Toss to coat. Marinate the beef, tossing once or twice, at room temperature for 1 hour or in the refrigerator for up to 8 hours. Remove the meat from the marinade, reserving the liquid.

4. In a wok or large skillet heat the oil over medium heat. Add the peppers, scallions and garlic and stir-fry until soft but not brown, 3 to 5 minutes. Remove the vegetables with a slotted spoon and reserve.

5. Add the meat to the wok and stir-fry until brown all over, 3 to 4 minutes.

6. **R**eturn the vegetables to the pan. Pour in the reserved marinade. Add the baby corn and snow peas. Cook, stirring, until the corn and sauce are hot and the snow peas are bright green, about 2 minutes. Mound the cooked rice on a large platter. Spoon the meat, vegetables and sauce on top.

Calories: 290	Protein: 20 gm	Total Fat: 9 gm
Saturated Fat: 3 gm	Cholesterol: 38 mg	Carbohydrates: 31 gm
Sodium: 450 mg	Dietary Fiber: 3 gm	

A SUPER SOURCE OF:

Phosphorus	28%
Vitamin B12	38%
Vitamin A	23%
Niacin	28%
Vitamin C	94%
Zinc	23%

0%   U.S. Recommended Daily Allowance   100%

Sweet corn provides significant amounts of thiamin, niacin and Vitamin C. It's rich in phosphorus and potassium, has respectable quantities of iron and zinc and is a good source of dietary fiber and protein.

A cup of fresh whole-kernel corn provides about 170 calories, with just 10 percent of those coming from fat. Carbohydrate content is about 38 grams; protein, 6 grams (nearly 10 percent of the adult Recommended Daily Allowance), and fat, 2 grams.

Corn is the most colorful of grains. Kernels can be yellow, white, red, brown, blue or mottled in any combination of these colors. Cobs can be white or red. Stalks, leaves and husks can be green, red, purple, brown, golden or even striped, while silk can be green, salmon or red.

*L*amb, Corn and Vegetable Kebabs

These flavorful kebabs can also be cooked on an outdoor grill following the same directions. Whether broiled or grilled, they're excellent for easy summertime entertaining. 4 SERVINGS

½ cup orange juice
2 tablespoons low-sodium soy sauce
2 tablespoons rice wine vinegar
3 scallions, chopped
1 garlic clove, minced
¼ teaspoon ground pepper
1 pound leg of lamb, cut into 1-inch cubes
1 medium zucchini, cut into 1-inch chunks
1 medium red bell pepper, cut into 1-inch pieces
1 medium green bell pepper, cut into 1-inch pieces
2 ears of fresh corn, cut into 1-inch pieces
1 large onion, cut into 12 wedges

1. In a medium bowl, combine the juice, soy sauce, vinegar, scallions, garlic and ground pepper. Whisk to blend. Pour the mixture into a heavy-duty plastic bag. Add the lamb cubes, turning them in the marinade to coat. Place the bag in the refrigerator for 1 hour, turning the bag over after 30 minutes.

2. Preheat the broiler. Lightly spray the broiler pan and 4 long metal skewers with vegetable cooking spray.

3. Remove the meat from the bag, reserving the marinade. Alternate pieces of lamb, zucchini, red and green bell peppers, corn and onion on the metal skewers. Place the kebabs in the prepared pan. Broil, basting and turning with the reserved marinade, until the lamb is pink and the vegetables are crisp-tender, 10 to 12 minutes.

Calories: 228	Protein: 59 gm	Total Fat: 6 gm
Saturated Fat: 2 gm	Cholesterol: 73 mg	Carbohydrates: 18 gm
Sodium: 381 mg	Dietary Fiber: 3 gm	

A SUPER SOURCE OF:

Phosphorus	▬▬▬▬ 30%
Thiamin	▬▬▬ 20%
Niacin	▬▬▬▬▬ 42%
Vitamin C	▬▬▬▬▬▬▬▬▬▬ 93%
Zinc	▬▬▬▬ 32%

0%   U.S. Recommended Daily Allowance   100%

Chicken Pozole

There are many variations of pozole, but the common ingredients are hominy, fish, meat or poultry, garlic, oregano, chiles and masa harina, a finely ground meal that acts as a corn thickener. Instead of browning the chicken in fat, this version calls for simmering the poultry in stock. Serve the pozole with wedges of lime and warm tortillas. 4 SERVINGS

1 tablespoon corn oil
3 scallions, chopped
1 medium green bell pepper, chopped
1 garlic clove, minced
4 cups chicken stock or canned low-sodium broth
1 pound boneless chicken breasts, cut into 2 × 3–inch pieces
2 tablespoons canned chopped green chiles
1 teaspoon chili powder
1 teaspoon oregano
½ teaspoon cumin
2 tablespoons masa harina
¼ cup cold water
1 can (16 ounces) whole yellow hominy, rinsed and drained

1. In a large skillet, heat the oil over medium heat. Add the scallions, bell pepper and garlic and cook until soft but not brown, 3 to 5 minutes.
2. Pour in the chicken stock and bring to a boil. Add the chicken, chiles, chili powder, oregano and cumin.
3. In a small bowl, combine the masa harina and cold water. Stir until smooth. Stir into the saucepan, blending until incorporated. Reduce the heat to low, cover and simmer until the chicken is tender, about 20 minutes.
4. Stir in the hominy and cook 5 minutes longer. Ladle into bowls.

Calories: 294	Protein: 31 gm	Total Fat: 8 gm
Saturated Fat: 1 gm	Cholesterol: 66 mg	Carbohydrates: 23 gm
Sodium: 374 mg	Dietary Fiber: 4 gm	

A SUPER SOURCE OF:

Phosphorus	28%
Niacin	74%
Vitamin C	70%

0%   U.S. Recommended Daily Allowance   100%

*P*ork with Hominy

6 SERVINGS

1 pound boneless pork loin chops, cut ½-inch thick
1 egg white, lightly beaten
½ cup yellow cornmeal
2 tablespoons olive oil
1 medium onion, chopped
1 cup beef stock or canned low-sodium broth
1 pound turnip greens, washed well and torn into pieces
1 can (16 ounces) yellow hominy, rinsed and drained
2 medium tomatoes, chopped (1 cup)
1 tablespoon chili powder
1 tablespoon cider vinegar
1 teaspoon salt
½ teaspoon pepper
¼ cup chopped cilantro or parsley

1. Dip the pork chops into the beaten egg white. Lightly coat with cornmeal. In a large skillet, heat 1 tablespoon of the olive oil over medium-high heat. Add the pork and cook until golden brown on the bottom, 5 to 7 minutes. Turn and cook until golden on the other side, 3 to 5 minutes; the pork will finish cooking later. Transfer the meat to a dish. Pour the fat from the pan and dry with a paper towel.

2. In the same pan, heat the remaining 1 tablespoon olive oil over medium heat. Add the onion and cook until soft but not brown, about 5 minutes. Add the stock, turnip greens, hominy, tomatoes, chili powder, vinegar, salt and pepper. Cover and cook 15 minutes.

3. Add the browned pork and accumulated juices to the pan. Bring to a boil. Reduce the heat to medium-low and simmer, covered, until the pork is tender, about 30 minutes. Add the cilantro and cook 5 minutes longer.

Calories: 314	Protein: 21 gm	Total Fat: 12 gm
Saturated Fat: 3 gm	Cholesterol: 48 mg	Carbohydrates: 31 gm
Sodium: 672 mg	Dietary Fiber: 6 gm	

A SUPER SOURCE OF:

Phosphorus	▬▬▬▬ 25%
Vitamin A	▬▬▬▬▬▬▬▬▬▬▬▬▬▬ 100%
Thiamin	▬▬▬▬▬▬▬▬▬ 71%
Niacin	▬▬▬▬ 26%
Vitamin C	▬▬▬▬▬▬▬▬▬▬▬▬▬ 92%

0%   U.S. Recommended Daily Allowance   100%

Corn Bread

This low-fat version of an American classic combines old-fashioned flavor with up-to-date ideas about healthy eating. Corn oil replaces the traditional melted shortening, two egg whites substitute for one whole egg, and buttermilk replaces whole milk.

MAKES 16 SQUARES

1¼ cups all-purpose flour
¾ cup yellow cornmeal
1 tablespoon baking powder
2 teaspoons sugar
¼ teaspoon salt
1¼ cups buttermilk
1 whole egg
2 egg whites
2 tablespoons corn oil

1. Preheat the oven to 400 degrees. Lightly coat an 8-inch cast-iron skillet or 8-inch square baking pan with vegetable cooking spray. If using the skillet, place it in the oven for 5 minutes to preheat while preparing the batter.

2. In a large bowl, combine the flour, cornmeal, baking powder, sugar and salt. Whisk gently to mix.

3. In another bowl, whisk together the buttermilk, whole egg, egg whites and oil. Add all at once to the dry ingredients. Stir only until moistened; the batter should be slightly lumpy.

4. Spoon the batter into the prepared skillet or pan and spread evenly to the edges with a rubber spatula. Bake 25 to 30 minutes, or until the top is golden and a toothpick inserted in the center comes out clean. Cut into 2-inch squares. Serve the corn bread warm.

Calories per square: 91	Protein: 3 gm	Total Fat: 2 gm
Saturated Fat: 0 gm	Cholesterol: 14 mg	Carbohydrates: 14 gm
Sodium: 145 mg	Dietary Fiber: 1 gm	

Cornmeal is made from what are called "dent" corns. These have kernels rich in soft starch that shrinks as it dries, leaving the end of each kernel with a characteristic "dent."

Very Corny Muffins

A triple dose of corn—cornmeal, fresh corn and corn oil— makes these muffins especially appealing. The yogurt contributes tang and moistness and helps reduce the fat. MAKES 12 MUFFINS

1¼ *cups all-purpose flour*
¾ *cup yellow cornmeal*
1 *tablespoon baking powder*
¼ *teaspoon salt*
1 *tablespoon maple syrup*
1¼ *cups nonfat plain yogurt*
1 *whole egg*
2 *egg whites*
2 *tablespoons corn oil*
½ *cup fresh corn kernels*

1. Preheat the oven to 400 degrees. Line a 12-count muffin tin with paper baking cups.

2. In a large bowl, combine the flour, cornmeal, baking powder and salt.

3. In another bowl, whisk together the maple syrup, yogurt, whole egg, egg whites and oil. Stir in the corn kernels. Add all at once to the dry ingredients. Stir only until moistened; the batter should be slightly lumpy.

4. Spoon the batter evenly into the prepared pan. Bake 20 to 25 minutes, or until the muffins are golden and springy to the touch. Remove the muffins from the pan and let cool on a wire rack.

Calories: 132 per muffin	Protein: 5 gm	Total Fat: 3 gm
Saturated Fat: 0 gm	Cholesterol: 18 mg	Carbohydrates: 21 gm
Sodium: 185 mg	Dietary Fiber: 1 gm	

Whole-grain cornmeal is a food packed with energy. A 1-ounce (¼ cup) portion provides 100 calories from 21 grams of carbohydrates, 2 grams of protein and 1 gram of fat.

Peach Cornmeal Pancakes

Any day that begins with these fruit-filled pancakes has got to be great. The cornmeal adds a slight crunch as well as a distinctive taste. 5 SERVINGS

1½ cups all-purpose flour
½ cup yellow cornmeal
1 tablespoon sugar
2 teaspoons baking powder
½ teaspoon baking soda
¼ teaspoon salt
1½ cups buttermilk
2 tablespoons sunflower or corn oil
1 whole egg, separated
2 egg whites
2 medium peaches, peeled and cut into ¼-inch dice

1. Lightly coat a large skillet or griddle with vegetable cooking spray.

2. In a large bowl, combine the flour, cornmeal, sugar, baking powder, baking soda and salt.

3. In a medium bowl, combine the buttermilk, oil and egg yolk. Whisk to blend. Add the liquid mixture to the dry mixture. Stir just until combined. In a dry clean bowl, beat the 3 egg whites until stiff. Fold into the batter. Gently stir in the diced peaches.

4. Drop about 3 tablespoons of the batter on the skillet for each pancake. Cook over medium heat until golden on the bottom with small bubbles on the top, 3 to 4 minutes. Turn and cook until golden on the other side, 1 to 2 minutes. Serve immediately.

Calories: 319	Protein: 10 gm	Total Fat: 8 gm
Saturated Fat: 1 gm	Cholesterol: 45 mg	Carbohydrates: 52 gm
Sodium: 473 mg	Dietary Fiber: 3 gm	

A SUPER SOURCE OF:

Thiamin ━━━━━━ 27%
Riboflavin ━━━━━━ 28%

0%   U.S. Recommended Daily Allowance   100%

Grits and cornmeal are much the same when it comes to calories. A 1-ounce (3 tablespoons) portion of enriched grits provides 100 calories from 22 grams of carbohydrate and 2 grams of protein.

*M*ushroom Corn Bread Dressing

This dressing flecked with vegetables can be served as a side dish year-round. It's also a wonderful stuffing for poultry or meat.

6 SERVINGS

2 tablespoons safflower oil
1 celery stalk, chopped
1 medium onion, chopped
1 medium green bell pepper, chopped
1/4 pound mushrooms, chopped
4 cups coarse corn bread crumbs (Corn Bread, p. 45.)
1 teaspoon sage
1/2 teaspoon salt
1/4 teaspoon pepper
1 1/2 cups chicken stock or canned low-sodium broth
1 egg

1. Preheat the oven to 350 degrees. Lightly coat a 1-quart casserole with vegetable cooking spray.

2. In a large skillet, heat the oil over medium heat. Add the celery, onion and bell pepper and cook until soft, 5 to 6 minutes. Add the mushrooms and cook until the liquid evaporates, about 5 minutes.

3. In a large bowl, place the corn bread crumbs, mushroom mixture, sage, salt and pepper. Add the stock and mix well. Blend in the egg.

4. Spoon the mixture into the prepared pan and spread to the edges with a rubber spatula. Cover with a lid or foil and bake for 20 minutes. Remove the cover and bake 15 minutes longer.

Calories: 317	Protein: 10 gm	Total Fat: 12 gm
Saturated Fat: 2 gm	Cholesterol: 73 mg	Carbohydrates: 41 gm
Sodium: 600 mg	Dietary Fiber: 2 gm	

A SUPER SOURCE OF:

Thiamin	━━━━━	21%
Riboflavin	━━━━━	23%
Vitamin C	━━━━━	31%

0%   U.S. Recommended Daily Allowance   100%

The Indians always knew just when to plant their corn: when the leaves on the oak trees were the size of squirrel's ears. By then, the soil was warm enough for the seeds to germinate properly.

*B*lueberry Corn Muffins

Frozen blueberries may be used in these fragrant orange-flavored muffins. Do not defrost the berries and they'll be just as tasty as the fresh ones. MAKES 12 MUFFINS

1¼ cups all-purpose flour
¾ cup yellow cornmeal
⅓ cup sugar
2 teaspoons baking powder
½ teaspoon baking soda
½ teaspoon grated orange zest
¼ teaspoon salt
1 egg
¾ cup skim milk
¼ cup orange juice
¼ cup safflower or vegetable oil
1 cup blueberries

1. Preheat the oven to 375 degrees. Line a 12-count muffin tin with paper baking cups.

2. In a large bowl, combine the flour, cornmeal, sugar, baking powder, baking soda, orange zest and salt. Whisk gently to mix.

3. In another bowl, combine the egg, milk, orange juice and oil. Whisk until well blended. Add all at once to the dry ingredients. Stir only until moistened; the batter should be slightly lumpy. Gently fold in the blueberries.

4. Spoon the batter evenly into the prepared pan. Bake 20 to 25 minutes, or until the muffins are golden and springy to the touch. Remove the muffins from the pan and let cool on a wire rack.

Calories per muffin: 162	Protein: 3 gm	Total Fat: 5 gm
Saturated Fat: 1 gm	Cholesterol: 18 mg	Carbohydrates: 25 gm
Sodium: 165 mg	Dietary Fiber: 1 gm	

Cranberry Corn Bread

Spangled with crimson-colored cranberries, this slightly sweet version of an American favorite would be perfect for Thanksgiving dinner. MAKES 9 SQUARES

¾ cup yellow cornmeal
1¼ cups all-purpose flour
⅓ cup sugar
2 teaspoons baking powder
½ teaspoon baking soda
2 teaspoons grated orange zest
¼ teaspoon salt
3 tablespoons canola or safflower oil
1½ cups buttermilk
¼ cup orange juice
1 egg
¾ cup coarsely chopped fresh or frozen cranberries

1. Preheat the oven to 400 degrees. Lightly coat an 8-inch square baking pan with vegetable cooking spray.

2. In a large bowl, combine the cornmeal, flour, sugar, baking powder, baking soda, orange zest and salt.

3. In a medium bowl, combine the oil, buttermilk, orange juice and egg. Whisk to blend well. Add to the dry ingredients and stir just until blended; the batter should be slightly lumpy. Fold in the cranberries.

4. Pour the batter evenly into the prepared pan and spread to the edges with a rubber spatula. Bake 30 to 35 minutes, or until a toothpick inserted in the center comes out clean. Cut into 9 squares. Serve warm or at room temperature.

Calories: 207 per square	Protein: 5 gm	Total Fat: 6 gm
Saturated Fat: 1 gm	Cholesterol: 25 mg	Carbohydrates: 34 gm
Sodium: 251 mg	Dietary Fiber: 1 gm	

Bluefish and Corn Salad with Spinach Dressing

In summer, when bluefish are plentiful, Americans along the Atlantic coast are always looking for new recipes for this full-flavored fish. 5 SERVINGS

1 pound small red potatoes, scrubbed
2 cups dry white wine
¾ pound bluefish fillets, ½ inch thick, skinned
2 cups cooked fresh corn kernels (from about 3 ears)
1 celery stalk, sliced
1 red onion, chopped
1 cup nonfat plain yogurt
1 tablespoon white wine vinegar
1 tablespoon olive oil, preferably extra virgin
1 tablespoon chopped fresh dill or 1 teaspoon dried
1 garlic clove, minced
½ teaspoon salt
¼ teaspoon pepper
⅛ teaspoon cayenne pepper
¼ pound fresh spinach leaves, washed well and drained, torn into bite-size pieces

1. In a large saucepan of boiling water, cook potatoes until tender, 20 to 25 minutes. Drain and let cool; then cut into quarters.
2. In a large noncorrosive skillet, heat the wine to boiling. Add the bluefish. Reduce the heat to a simmer, partially cover the pan and cook until the fish is firm and opaque throughout, 10 to 12 minutes. Remove the fish from the pan. Let cool, then break into 1-inch chunks.
3. In a large salad bowl, combine the bluefish, corn, potatoes, celery and onion.
4. Prepare a dressing by whisking together the yogurt, vinegar, oil, dill, garlic, salt, pepper and cayenne in a medium bowl. Stir in the spinach. Pour the dressing over the salad and toss.

Calories: 292	Protein: 21 gm	Total Fat: 7 gm
Saturated Fat: 1 gm	Cholesterol: 41 mg	Carbohydrates: 39 gm
Sodium: 339 mg	Dietary Fiber: 5 gm	

A SUPER SOURCE OF:

Vitamin B12	66%
Vitamin A	39%
Niacin	35%
Vitamin C	45%

0%   U.S. Recommended Daily Allowance   100%

*P*eppery Corn Sticks

A little butter plus lots of naturally lean buttermilk make these corn sticks rich and moist, yet with very little fat. MAKES 12 CORN STICKS

1 cup yellow cornmeal
1 cup all-purpose flour
2 tablespoons sugar
2 teaspoons baking powder
¼ teaspoon salt
3 tablespoons unsalted butter, melted
1 small red bell pepper, chopped
1 small green bell pepper, chopped
1¼ cups buttermilk
1 whole egg
2 egg whites
½ cup fresh or frozen corn kernels

1. Preheat the oven to 400 degrees. Lightly coat a 12-count corn stick pan or a 9-inch square baking pan with vegetable cooking spray.

2. In a large bowl, combine the cornmeal, flour, sugar, baking powder and salt. Whisk gently to mix.

3. In a large skillet, heat 1 tablespoon melted butter. Add the red and green peppers and cook over medium heat until softened, about 3 minutes. Remove from the heat.

4. In a medium bowl, mix together the buttermilk, remaining 2 tablespoons melted butter, whole egg and egg whites. Add the cooked peppers and the corn kernels. Pour into the dry ingredients and stir just until combined.

5. Pour into the prepared pan and quickly spread to the edges with a rubber spatula. Bake 20 to 25 minutes, or until a toothpick inserted in the center comes out clean. If baking in a 9-inch square pan, increase the baking time to 30 to 35 minutes and cut into 12 pieces after baking.

Calories: 142 per corn stick	Protein: 4 gm	Total Fat: 4 gm
Saturated Fat: 2 gm	Cholesterol: 26 mg	Carbohydrates: 22 gm
Sodium: 160 mg	Dietary Fiber: 1 gm	

A SUPER SOURCE OF:
Vitamin C ━━━━━━ 26%

0%   U.S. Recommended Daily Allowance   100%

*B*aked Polenta with Chunky Tomato Sauce

Polenta is yellow cornmeal cooked Italian-style. To prepare it for baking, this thick corn porridge is spread in a pan and refrigerated until firm. In this recipe, squares of cold polenta are sautéed in olive oil until golden, topped with tomato sauce and cheese, and baked until bubbling hot. 9 SERVINGS

4½ cups water
2 cups yellow cornmeal
2 teaspoons olive oil, preferably extra virgin
¾ cup Chunky Tomato Sauce (recipe follows)
¼ cup shredded part-skim mozzarella cheese
¼ cup grated Parmesan cheese

1. Lightly coat a 9-inch square baking pan with vegetable cooking spray.
2. In a medium saucepan, heat the water to boiling over high heat. Gradually stir in 1½ cups cornmeal. Reduce the heat to a simmer and cook, stirring, until the mixture is very thick, 12 to 15 minutes. Spread the polenta into the prepared pan and refrigerate, covered, until thoroughly chilled and firm, about 3 hours. Cut into 3-inch squares.
3. Preheat the oven to 350 degrees. Lightly coat a 10 × 14–inch baking pan with vegetable cooking spray. Place the remaining ½ cup of cornmeal in a shallow dish. Pat both sides of the polenta squares with the remaining ½ cup cornmeal. In a large skillet, heat the olive oil over medium heat. Add the polenta squares and cook until golden brown on the bottom, 3 to 5 minutes. Turn and cook until golden on the other side, about 3 minutes.
4. Place the polenta squares into the prepared pan. Top with Chunky Tomato Sauce. Sprinkle the mozzarella and Parmesan cheese over the sauce. Bake until the polenta is heated through and the cheese has melted, about 7 minutes. Pass the remaining tomato sauce on the side.

Calories: 168   Protein: 5 gm   Total Fat: 4 gm
Cholesterol: 4 mg   Carbohydrates: 28 gm   Sodium: 269 mg
Dietary Fiber: 2 gm

A SUPER SOURCE OF:
Vitamin A ━━━━━━━━━━━━━━━ 57%

0%   U.S. Recommended Daily Allowance   100%

Chunky Tomato Sauce

MAKES 1¾ CUPS

2 teaspoons olive oil, preferably extra virgin
1 medium onion, chopped
1 garlic clove, minced
1 carrot, grated
1 can (16 ounces) crushed tomatoes, with their juice
2 tablespoons chopped fresh basil
2 tablespoons chopped fresh parsley
1 teaspoon dried oregano
½ teaspoon salt
¼ teaspoon pepper
¼ teaspoon crushed hot pepper flakes

1. In a medium saucepan, heat the olive oil over medium heat. Add the onion, garlic and carrot and cook until soft but not brown, about 5 minutes.

2. Add the tomatoes with their juice, basil, parsley, oregano, salt, pepper and hot pepper flakes. Reduce the heat to a simmer and cook, partially covered, 45 minutes.

Calories: 64 per ½ cup	Protein: 2 gm	Total Fat: 3 gm
Saturated Fat: 0 gm	Cholesterol: 0 mg	Carbohydrates: 10 gm
Sodium: 477 mg	Dietary Fiber: 2 gm	

A SUPER SOURCE OF:

Vitamin A ▬▬▬▬▬▬▬▬▬▬▬▬▬▬ 100%
Vitamin C ▬▬▬▬▬ 40%

0%   U.S. Recommended Daily Allowance   100%

Cornmeal Waffles

These waffles are crisp and crunchy outside, tender inside. Pure maple syrup is the perfect topping. 5 SERVINGS

1¼ cups all-purpose flour
¾ cup yellow cornmeal
1 tablespoon sugar
2 teaspoons baking powder
½ teaspoon baking soda
¼ teaspoon salt
2 tablespoons canola or safflower oil
1¾ cups buttermilk
1 egg

1. Preheat and lightly coat a waffle iron with vegetable cooking spray.
2. In a large bowl, combine the flour, cornmeal, sugar, baking powder, baking soda and salt. Whisk gently to mix.
3. In another bowl, thoroughly combine the oil, buttermilk and egg. Whisk to blend. Add to the dry ingredients and stir until just blended; the batter should be slightly lumpy.
4. Pour about ⅓ cup of the batter onto the prepared waffle iron and cook about 4 to 5 minutes, or until golden brown and crisp. Repeat with the remaining batter. Serve the waffles immediately with fresh fruit or drizzled with maple syrup.

Calories: 298	Protein: 9 gm	Total Fat: 8 gm
Cholesterol: 46 mg	Carbohydrates: 47 gm	Sodium: 464 mg
Dietary Fiber: 2 gm		

A SUPER SOURCE OF:

Calcium	▬▬▬▬	20%
Thiamin	▬▬▬▬▬	27%
Riboflavin	▬▬▬▬	24%

0%   U.S. Recommended Daily Allowance   100%

*G*rits *Soufflé*

This combination of mild-mannered grits and three kinds of hot peppers is a study in contrasts that works beautifully. 4 SERVINGS

2 teaspoons safflower oil
1 jalapeño pepper, seeded and chopped
1 garlic clove, minced
3 drops of hot pepper sauce
⅛ teaspoon cayenne pepper
¼ teaspoon ground black pepper
2 cups skim milk
½ cup grits
⅓ cup reduced-sodium Cheddar cheese
2 egg whites
1 whole egg, separated

1. Preheat the oven to 350 degrees. Lightly coat a 1-quart deep baking dish or soufflé pan with vegetable cooking spray.

2. In a small skillet, heat the oil over medium heat. Add the jalapeño pepper and garlic and cook until soft but not brown, about 3 minutes. Add the hot sauce, cayenne pepper and black pepper. Cook 1 minute longer. Remove the pan from the heat and let cool for 10 minutes.

3. In a medium saucepan, cook the milk over medium heat until boiling. Gradually stir in the grits. Cook, stirring, until thickened, 8 to 10 minutes. Blend in the cheese and pepper-garlic mixture. Set the soufflé base aside.

4. In a clean, dry bowl, whip the 3 egg whites until stiff. Whisk the egg yolk into the soufflé base. Fold in the beaten egg whites. Bake 30 minutes, or until puffed and golden. Serve immediately.

Calories: 205	Protein: 12 gm	Total Fat: 7 gm
Saturated Fat: 1 gm	Cholesterol: 54 mg	Carbohydrates: 23 gm
Sodium: 142 mg	Dietary Fiber: 0 gm	

A SUPER SOURCE OF:

Calcium	━━━━━━	25%
Riboflavin	━━━━━	22%

0%   U.S. Recommended Daily Allowance   100%

FEELING YOUR OATS

When Samuel Johnson wrote the first English dictionary more than two centuries ago, he sneeringly defined oats as "a grain which is generally given to horses, but in Scotland supports the people." Dr. Johnson may have known the English language and his own prejudices, but he was no expert on nutrition. Among common grains, oats are one of the highest in nutritional value, with protein content averaging about 14 percent. Oats are also rich in minerals, Vitamin E, several B vitamins and both soluble and insoluble fiber.

Scotland without oatmeal is unthinkable, and in this country, oatmeal was the one form of the grain everyone knew before 1988. Since then oat bran has also become a familiar product on the American market, thanks mostly to the mass media, which ballyhooed a 1988 American Medical Association report suggesting that a diet high in dietary fiber, including oat bran, might help reduce blood cholesterol in some individuals. (For more bran information and recipes, see pages 92–103.)

In the United States, oats are the one grain commonly consumed whole or just slightly processed. The grain is threshed to remove the inedible outer husks, but the bran and germ are left intact. Whole oats can take up to 2 hours to cook. Reducing the grain to some kind of meal greatly reduces that time. Oatmeal has much the same nutritional profile as whole oats, but cooking times vary significantly with type.

▲ **Steel-cut oats,** also known as Scottish or Irish oatmeal, are the least-processed form of oatmeal. The only thing done to the oats is to slice them lengthwise with sharp steel blades so they'll cook in about 40 minutes. Porridge made with steel-cut oats is thick, chewy and satisfying.

▲ **Rolled "old-fashioned" oats** are oats that have been softened slightly by steaming, then flattened between steel rollers. They cook in a fraction of the time required for steel-cut oats—little more than 5 minutes.

▲ **Rolled "quick-cooking" oats** are oats that are steamed and cut into three or four slices before being flattened by rollers. This reduces the cooking time to little more than 1 minute.

▲ **"Instant" oatmeal** is rolled very thin, precooked, then dehydrated. The oats are rehydrated "instantly" by adding boiling water. Instant oatmeals are often packaged with flavorings, sugar and salt included.

Oats are much more than just a breakfast cereal, however. Whole oats can be used in grain salads and added to soup, like barley. Here cooking time is only an hour or so, depending on the degree of tenderness desired. Rolled oats, old-fashioned or quick-cooking, can be used as a meat extender in meat loaf and burgers, and either can be used for cookies.

In many baked-goods recipes — muffins and quick breads, particularly — up to one third of the wheat flour can be replaced by oat flour or by rolled oats that have been ground to fine meal in a food processor. In yeast breads, up to one fifth of the wheat flour can be replaced by oat flour or fine meal, and the two can be substituted for all-purpose flour one for one when thickening soups and sauces or when coating fish, chicken and the like before frying or baking.

Oats and oat flour keep well in storage (in an airtight container in a cool cupboard) because oats contain a natural antioxidant that can prevent the grain from going stale for many months.

To cook whole oats, use 2 cups water, 1 cup whole oats and a heavy pot with a cover. Bring water to a boil, stir in oats, reduce heat to a simmer and cover tightly. Cooking takes 1 to 2 hours, depending on the degree of tenderness desired. After 1 hour, the grains will still be quite firm and are good for salads. After 2 hours, the grains will burst and become very soft, which is best for breakfast cereal.

A to *Z* Oat Muffins

From apple to zucchini, these muffins are packed with nutritious, flavorful ingredients. Great for breakfast, they're low in fat and filling. MAKES 12 MUFFINS

1¼ cups all-purpose flour
½ cup regular or quick-cooking oats
2 teaspoons baking powder
½ teaspoon baking soda
1 teaspoon cinnamon
⅓ cup packed brown sugar
¼ cup safflower oil
1 egg
1 tart-sweet cooking apple, such as Granny Smith, peeled and shredded
1 medium zucchini, grated

1. **P**reheat the oven to 375 degrees. Line a 12-count muffin tin with paper baking cups.

2. **I**n a medium bowl, combine the flour, oats, baking powder, baking soda and cinnamon.

3. **I**n a large bowl, combine the brown sugar, oil and egg. Whisk until well blended. Stir in the apple and zucchini. Add all at once to the dry ingredients. Stir only until moistened; the batter should be slightly lumpy.

4. **S**poon the batter evenly into the prepared pan. Bake 20 to 25 minutes, or until the muffins are golden and springy to the touch. Remove the muffins from the pan and let cool on a wire rack.

Calories: 138 per muffin	Protein: 3 gm	Total Fat: 5 gm
Saturated Fat: 1 gm	Cholesterol: 18 mg	Carbohydrates: 20 gm
Sodium: 113 mg	Dietary Fiber: 1 gm	

To make porridge with "old-fashioned" rolled oats, use 2 to 2½ cups water to 1 cup oats. Sprinkle oats over briskly boiling water, reduce heat slightly and cook 5 minutes, stirring occasionally. Cover, remove from heat and let stand a few minutes until the mixture has thickened to the desired consistency. This makes 2 to 3 servings.

*T*wice-Baked Walnut Oat Cookies

In Italy, these not-too-sweet cookies are called *biscotti*. They are very crunchy because of the second baking, and they are ideal for dunking. MAKES 40 COOKIES

⅓ cup chopped walnuts
1 whole egg
2 egg whites
⅓ cup walnut or safflower oil
⅓ cup sugar
¼ cup orange juice
½ teaspoon almond extract
1 cup all-purpose flour
¾ cup regular or quick-cooking oats
⅓ cup whole wheat flour
¼ cup cornstarch
2 teaspoons grated orange zest
2 teaspoons baking powder
1½ teaspoons cinnamon
½ teaspoon nutmeg
⅛ teaspoon salt

1. Preheat the oven to 325 degrees. Spread out the walnuts on a small baking sheet. Bake until barely toasted, about 6 to 8 minutes. Remove them from the pan and cool completely on a paper towel. Turn off the oven.

2. In a large bowl, using a hand-held electric mixer, beat the whole egg, egg whites, oil, sugar, orange juice and almond extract at medium speed for 5 minutes, or until light.

3. Add the all-purpose flour, oats, whole wheat flour, cornstarch, orange zest, baking powder, cinnamon, nutmeg and salt. Reduce the speed to low and mix just until combined. (This is a sticky dough.) Stir in the toasted nuts. Remove the dough from the bowl and wrap it in plastic wrap. Refrigerate for 1 hour.

4. Preheat the oven to 350 degrees. Lightly coat a cookie sheet with vegetable cooking spray.

5. Divide the dough into 3 sections. On a lightly floured board, shape each section into a 10 × 1–inch log. Place the logs onto the prepared pan, spacing them 2 inches apart. Bake 25 minutes. Remove the pan from the oven, but leave the oven on.

6. Transfer the baked logs to a cutting board with a spatula. Cut each log into ¾-inch diagonal slices. Return the pieces to the cookie sheet and bake 10 minutes longer. Remove the cookies from the pan and cool on a wire rack.

Calories per cookie: 56	Protein: 1 gm	Total Fat: 3 gm
Saturated Fat: 0 gm	Cholesterol: 5 mg	Carbohydrates: 7 gm
Sodium: 33 mg	Dietary Fiber: 0 gm	

Easy Oat-Raisin Bread

Making yeast bread dough in a food processor is a magical experience. First-time bread bakers are usually amazed at the speed and ease of preparation. This majestic bread is a real winner in taste and appearance. MAKES 1 LOAF, 16 SLICES

½ cup warm water (105 to 115 degrees)
1 tablespoon honey
1 envelope active dry yeast
1 cup skim milk
4 tablespoons unsalted butter, cut into pieces, softened
⅓ cup raisins
¼ cup orange juice
1½ teaspoons grated orange zest
2 teaspoons cinnamon
2½ to 3 cups bread flour
¾ cup regular or quick-cooking oats
½ teaspoon salt
2 tablespoons sugar
1 egg white, lightly beaten

1. Place the water and honey in a small bowl. Stir in the yeast. Let the mixture stand until foamy, about 5 minutes.

2. In a small saucepan, heat the milk and butter, stirring, until the mixture is warm and the butter has melted. Remove the pan from the heat.

3. Place the raisins in a small bowl. Add the orange juice, zest and 1 teaspoon cinnamon. Mix to combine.

4. In a food processor fitted with the metal blade, place 2½ cups of the bread flour, the oats and the salt. With the machine on, add the yeast mixture and the warmed milk and butter through the feed tube. When it forms a ball, process it 45 seconds longer, until the dough is smooth and elastic. If the dough is too wet and doesn't form a ball, gradually add the remaining ⅓ cup of bread flour, 1 tablespoon at a time.

5. Lightly spray a large bowl with vegetable cooking spray. Place the dough in the bowl and turn to coat evenly. Loosely cover the dough and let rise in a warm draft-free place for 1 hour, or until it is doubled in size.

6. Thoroughly drain the raisins on a double thickness of paper or cotton towels, gently pressing out any liquid.

7. Lightly flour a wooden board. Knead the raisins into the dough until distributed evenly throughout. Roll the dough into a 10 × 15–inch rectangle. Sprinkle with the sugar and remaining 1 teaspoon cinnamon. Beginning with a short end, roll up the dough. Pinch the ends and seam together to seal. Lightly coat a 9 × 5 × 3–inch loaf pan with vegetable cooking spray. Place the dough, seam side down, in the prepared pan. Loosely cover the dough and let rise 45 minutes, or until it is almost doubled in size. Preheat the oven to 400 degrees.

8. **B**rush the top of the dough with the egg white. Bake 30 to 35 minutes, or until the crust is golden and the bottom sounds hollow when tapped. Remove the loaf from the pan and cool on a wire rack.

Calories per slice: 154	Protein: 4 gm	Total Fat: 3 gm
Saturated Fat: 2 gm	Cholesterol: 8 mg	Carbohydrates: 26 gm
Sodium: 81 mg	Dietary Fiber: 1 gm	

The nutritional values of whole and steel-cut oats and oat flour are essentially the same as those for rolled oats. One-ounce portions are as follows: whole oats, 2 tablespoons uncooked; steel-cut oats, 2½ tablespoons uncooked; oat flour, 2½ tablespoons.

*A*pple Cranberry Crisp with Crunchy Oat Topping

This dessert is perfect in the fall when apples and cranberries are plentiful. It can be prepared all year long if you buy several bags of cranberries when you see them at the market and freeze them for future use. 5 SERVINGS

¾ cup sugar
¼ cup unsweetened apple juice
½ cup coarsely chopped cranberries
4 sweet apples, such as Delicious, peeled and cut into ½-inch dice
½ cup regular or quick-cooking oats
¼ cup all-purpose flour
1½ teaspoons grated orange zest
1 teaspoon cinnamon
½ teaspoon nutmeg
2 tablespoons unsalted soft butter, cut into ½-inch slices

1. Preheat oven to 350 degrees. Lightly coat a 9-inch square baking pan with vegetable cooking spray.

2. In a small saucepan, place ½ cup sugar and the apple juice. Bring to a boil, stirring to dissolve the sugar. Add the cranberries. Reduce the heat to a simmer, cover and cook until the cranberries are just tender and the skins begin to pop, about 5 minutes. Remove the pan from the heat. Place the cranberries and juice into a small bowl and refrigerate for 30 minutes.

3. Place the apples in the prepared pan. Top with the cranberry mixture.

4. In a medium bowl, combine the oats, flour, ¼ cup sugar, orange zest, cinnamon and nutmeg. Cut in the butter with a pastry blender or 2 knives until crumbly and the consistency is that of coarse meal. Sprinkle over the fruit in the pan. Bake 30 to 35 minutes, until the apples are tender and the topping is golden. Serve the crisp warm or at room temperature.

Calories: 289	Protein: 2 gm	Total Fat: 6 gm
Saturated Fat: 3 gm	Cholesterol: 12 mg	Carbohydrates: 60 gm
Sodium: 2 gm	Dietary Fiber: 3 gm	

A SUPER SOURCE OF:
Vitamin C ━━━━━ 23%

0%   U.S. Recommended Daily Allowance   100%

Granola Squares

These bars are great as part of a breakfast or after-school snack.

MAKES 36 SQUARES

1 cup Almond Granola (see p. 65)
1 cup all-purpose flour
⅔ cup whole wheat flour
¼ cup sugar
2 teaspoons baking powder
½ teaspoon baking soda
¼ teaspoon salt
1½ cups buttermilk
¼ cup safflower oil
1 egg

1. Preheat the oven to 350 degrees. Lightly coat a 9-inch square baking pan with vegetable cooking spray.

2. In a large bowl, combine the Almond Granola, all-purpose flour, whole wheat flour, sugar, baking powder, baking soda and salt.

3. In a medium bowl, place the buttermilk, oil and egg. Whisk until well blended. Add all at once to the dry ingredients. Stir only until moistened; the batter should be slightly lumpy.

4. Spread the batter evenly into the prepared pan. Bake 25 to 30 minutes, or until the top is golden and a toothpick inserted in the center comes out clean. Cool in the pan on a wire rack before cutting into 1½-inch squares.

Calories: 68 per square	Protein: 2 gm	Total Fat: 3 gm
Saturated Fat: 0 gm	Cholesterol: 6 mg	Carbohydrates: 9 gm
Sodium: 63 mg	Dietary Fiber: 1 gm	

To make Scottish- or Irish-style porridge, use 4 cups water, 1 cup steel-cut oats and a heavy pot. Sprinkle oats over rapidly boiling water, reduce heat slightly and cook until porridge begins to thicken. Reduce heat to a simmer and cook about 30 minutes, stirring occasionally. This will make 3 to 4 servings of thick, chewy, satisfying porridge.

*A*lmond Granola

The flavor of almonds comes through twice in this crunchy, fruit-packed cereal. The mixture is also a major ingredient in the Granola Squares (p. 64). 6 SERVINGS

2 cups regular or quick-cooking oats
⅓ cup sunflower seeds
¼ cup slivered almonds
2 tablespoons wheat germ
¼ cup sunflower or safflower oil
¼ cup honey
¼ cup unsweetened apple juice
½ teaspoon almond extract
¼ cup chopped dried apricots
¼ cup chopped prunes
¼ cup raisins

1. Preheat the oven to 250 degrees. Lightly coat a 9 × 13–inch baking pan with vegetable cooking spray.

2. In a large bowl, combine the oats, sunflower seeds, almonds and wheat germ.

3. In a small bowl, combine the oil, honey, apple juice and almond extract. Whisk until blended. Pour the liquid mixture over the dry ingredients. Stir until incorporated.

4. Spread into the prepared pan. Bake 45 minutes, stirring every 15 minutes. Mix in the apricots, prunes and raisins. Bake 15 minutes longer. Cool the granola completely before storing in a tightly covered container.

Calories: 368	Protein: 8 gm	Total Fat: 18 gm
Saturated Fat: 2 gm	Cholesterol: 0 mg	Carbohydrates: 47 gm
Sodium: 4 mg	Dietary Fiber: 5 gm	

A SUPER SOURCE OF:

Phosphorus ▬▬▬▬ 26%
Thiamin ▬▬▬▬ 27%

0%   U.S. Recommended Daily Allowance   100%

> *A 1-ounce serving of rolled oats (⅓ cup uncooked, ⅔ cup cooked) provides 100 calories from 19 grams of carbohydrates, 4 grams of protein and 2 grams of fat. The carbohydrates include 3 grams of dietary fiber.*

Carrot Pineapple Oat Snacking Cake

With buttermilk and pineapple contributing moistness and flavor, this carrot cake needs no icing. Zucchini can be used in place of the carrots for equally delicious results. MAKES 16 SQUARES

¾ cup all-purpose flour
½ cup regular or quick-cooking oats
¼ cup whole wheat flour
⅓ cup packed brown sugar
2 teaspoons baking powder
2 teaspoons cinnamon
½ teaspoon mace
⅛ teaspoon salt
¾ cup buttermilk
¼ cup safflower oil
1 whole egg
2 egg whites
1 cup grated carrots
1 can (8 ounces) unsweetened crushed pineapple, juice reserved

1. Preheat the oven to 375 degrees. Lightly coat an 8-inch square baking pan with vegetable cooking spray.

2. In a large bowl, combine the all-purpose flour, oats, whole wheat flour, brown sugar, baking powder, cinnamon, mace and salt.

3. In a medium bowl, combine the buttermilk, oil, whole egg and the egg whites. Whisk until well blended. Stir in the carrots and the pineapple with its juice. Add the flour mixture to the liquid ingredients. Stir just until combined.

4. Spread the batter into the prepared pan. Bake 30 to 35 minutes, or until a toothpick inserted in the center comes out clean. Cool the cake in the pan on a wire rack. Cut into 2-inch squares.

Calories: 111 per square	Protein: 3 gm	Total Fat: 4 gm
Saturated Fat: 0 gm	Cholesterol: 14 mg	Carbohydrates: 16 gm
Sodium: 98 mg	Dietary Fiber: 1 gm	

A SUPER SOURCE OF:
Vitamin A ▬▬▬▬▬▬ 39%

0%   U.S. Recommended Daily Allowance   100%

*A*lmond-Oat Meringue Drops

These light cookies melt in your mouth. Toasting the oats, wheat germ and almonds intensifies the flavor. MAKES 34 MERINGUE COOKIES

¼ cup regular or quick-cooking oats
¼ cup wheat germ
¼ cup slivered almonds
2 egg whites
⅓ cup sugar
1 teaspoon almond extract

1. Preheat the oven to 325 degrees. On a small baking sheet, spread out the oats, wheat germ and almonds. Bake until barely toasted, 6 to 8 minutes. Remove from the pan and cool completely on a paper towel.

2. Lower the oven temperature to 275 degrees. Lightly coat a cookie sheet with vegetable cooking spray.

3. In a medium bowl, using a hand-held electric mixer, beat the egg whites at high speed until soft peaks form, 3 to 4 minutes. Gradually add the sugar and beat until stiff. Add the almond extract. Fold in the toasted wheat germ, oats and almonds.

4. Using 2 tablespoons, spoon the batter evenly onto the prepared pan, leaving a 1-inch space between the unbaked meringues. Bake 24 to 28 minutes, or until the meringues are set and barely colored. Remove the meringues from the pan and cool on a wire rack.

Calories per meringue: 20	Protein: 1 gm	Total Fat: 1 gm
Saturated Fat: 0 gm	Cholesterol: 0 mg	Carbohydrates: 3 gm
Sodium: 3 mg	Dietary Fiber: .2 gm	

*C*rispy *Deviled Chicken Drumsticks*

When the word "deviled" appears in a recipe, that's a sure sign that one of the main ingredients is mustard. Two kinds of mustard flavor this assertive chicken dish. 4 SERVINGS

½ cup regular or quick-cooking oats
1 tablespoon safflower oil
4 drops of hot pepper sauce
¼ cup coarse grainy mustard
3 tablespoons Dijon mustard
2 scallions, chopped
1 tablespoon white wine vinegar
¼ teaspoon salt
¼ teaspoon pepper
6 chicken drumsticks about 4 ounces each, skin removed
½ cup coarse whole wheat bread crumbs

1. Preheat the oven to 350 degrees. Lightly coat an 8-inch square baking pan with vegetable cooking spray.

2. Place the oats in a small baking pan. Bake until the oats begin to turn light brown in color, about 10 minutes. Stir and bake 23 minutes longer. Remove the oats from the pan and let cool.

3. In a small bowl, combine the oil, hot sauce, grainy mustard, Dijon mustard, scallions, vinegar, salt and pepper. With a pastry brush, coat both sides of the chicken with the mixture.

4. Place the bread crumbs and the toasted oats in a shallow dish. Toss to mix. Pat the crumbs onto both sides of the chicken. Bake 45 minutes, or until the juices run clear when the leg is pricked and the chicken is crisp and golden brown on top.

Calories: 349	Protein: 43 gm	Total Fat: 13 gm
Saturated Fat: 2 gm	Cholesterol: 156 mg	Carbohydrates: 13 gm
Sodium: 826 mg	Dietary Fiber: 2 gm	

A SUPER SOURCE OF:

Phosphorus	39%
Riboflavin	23%
Niacin	60%
Zinc	29%

0%   U.S. Recommended Daily Allowance   100%

*M*arvelous *Meat Loaf*

What tastes better—hot meat loaf fresh from the oven or leftover meat loaf, cold and sandwiched between slices of whole wheat bread for lunch the next day? You be the judge. 4 SERVINGS

2 teaspoons safflower or vegetable oil
1 medium onion, minced
1 pound lean ground turkey
1 egg white
1 carrot, grated
½ cup no-salt-added tomato juice
½ teaspoon salt
¼ teaspoon pepper
½ cup regular or quick-cooking oats
¼ cup water

1. Preheat the oven to 350 degrees. Lightly coat a 9-inch square baking pan with vegetable cooking spray.

2. In a medium skillet, heat the oil over medium heat. Add the onion and cook until soft but not brown, 3 to 4 minutes. Transfer the onion to a medium bowl and let cool slightly, about 10 minutes.

3. Add the ground turkey, egg white, carrot, tomato juice, salt and pepper. Mix well.

4. In a small bowl, combine the oats and water. Add to the turkey mixture and mix to blend well. Shape the meat into a loaf in the prepared pan. Bake 1 hour.

Calories: 246	Protein: 23 gm	Total Fat: 12 gm
Saturated Fat: 3 gm	Cholesterol: 83 mg	Carbohydrates: 12 gm
Sodium: 404 mg	Dietary Fiber: 2 gm	

A SUPER SOURCE OF:

Phosphorus ▬▬▬▬ 25%
Vitamin A ▬▬▬▬▬▬▬▬▬▬▬▬▬▬▬▬▬▬ 100%
Niacin ▬▬▬ 22%

0%   U.S. Recommended Daily Allowance   100%

GET RAVES WITH RICE

Rice is the "daily bread" of more than half the human race. Native to Africa, India and Indochina, this delicately flavored grain is now grown in tropical to temperate regions around the world. Some 40,000 varieties are in cultivation today, but the cook usually has to consider only two things: What's the length of the grains and how have they been processed? Long and medium are the two most common lengths, and the two are different in the package, the cooking pot and on the plate.

A kernel of long-grain rice is four to five times longer than it is wide. When cooked, the grains are fluffy and separate. This rice is tops for serving plain and in salads, casseroles and other dishes where a firmer, more distinct rice texture is a plus. Our Stir-Fried Chicken with Rice and Peanuts, and Stuffed Peppers show off the versatility of long-grain rice.

Medium-grain rice is shorter and plumper than long-grain rice. When cooked, the grains are moister and more tender, with a greater tendency to stick together or "clump." Medium-grain rice is ideal for rice pudding, risottos and any dish where a smoother consistency is desired. Our Risotto Verde, Smoked Turkey Risotto, and Risotto with Fresh Peas gain extra-creamy texture from Arborio rice, a special medium-grain variety imported from Italy.

As rice grows, each grain is enclosed in an inedible husk, so all rice has to go through a certain amount of processing or milling before it can be eaten. Brown rice is the least processed. The inedible outer husk has been removed, but otherwise the grain is the way nature made it. Layers of bran clinging to each grain give brown rice a tawny hue and extra nutritional value. That bran, however, contains a trace of oil that can go rancid, so it's best to store brown rice in the refrigerator or to buy it in a modest quantity and use it before it goes stale.

Cooked brown rice has a nutty flavor and a slightly chewy texture, qualities that come to the fore in the recipes we've provided. East (rice and tofu) meets West (turkey, tomatoes and pinto beans) in Turkey Tofu Chili with Brown Rice. Apricot and Pecan Brown Rice can be prepared as a side dish or used to stuff a chicken. Chicken Stuffed with Broccoli and Brown Rice illustrates how healthy eating and good taste can go hand in hand.

White rice has been milled, or polished, to remove the bran layers from the outside of the grain, giving white rice a more delicate flavor and indefinite shelf life. Milling, however, does remove the nutrients found in the bran, so most white rice is enriched with iron and the B vitamins niacin and thiamin to replace the most important of the lost nutrients. After milling, white rice is often coated with glucose or vegetable oil to give it greater sheen.

Parboiled or "converted" rice is soaked in water, steamed, dried and, finally, polished. This process dissolves some of the nutrients in the bran and soaks them into the grain, which in most cases is also enriched. Parboiling is not a form of precooking, however. After the process, the grain is harder than ordinary milled rice and requires a few minutes more cooking time and a greater amount of liquid. The rice does turn out fluffier and more separate, which make it a good choice for salads and dishes that will be reheated.

Precooked or "instant" rice is milled, completely cooked and dried. This rice takes the least time to prepare, but its texture is quite different from that of ordinary and parboiled rices.

Aromatic rices are relatively new on the American market, but they've been around for centuries. The most celebrated aromatic variety is the Basmati rice of northern India and Pakistan, which has a subtle nutlike flavor. An American-bred Basmati hybrid called Texmati is now widely available. Popcorn-scented rice is sold under a number of brand names; Jasmine, Wehani and Wild Pecan are yet other scented varieties. Native American "wild rice," with its dark, inch-long seeds, is not a variety of rice at all. It comes from another grass species that, confusingly, is sometimes called wild oats.

> *Archaeological evidence suggests that rice was in cultivation in Thailand by 3,500 B.C. It reached America in the late 1600s, and many superb American dishes feature the grain, particularly in the southern, Creole and Cajun traditions.*

*C*reamy *Carrot Rice Soup*

Most of the rice is pureed to make this a thick "cream soup" without a drop of cream. Pureed cooked rice can be substituted for cream in just about any cream soup recipe, putting these lovely soups back into the healthy category. 5 SERVINGS

2 tablespoons safflower oil
1 medium onion, coarsely chopped
3 medium carrots, coarsely chopped
½ cup long-grained white rice
3 cups chicken stock or canned low-sodium broth
½ cup evaporated skimmed milk
1 teaspoon salt
¼ teaspoon pepper
¼ teaspoon nutmeg

1. In a large saucepan, heat the oil. Add the onion and carrots and cook over medium heat until the onions are soft and the carrots are crisp-tender, about 8 minutes.

2. Add the rice and chicken stock. Bring to a boil. Reduce the heat to a simmer, cover and cook until the rice is tender, 18 to 20 minutes.

3. With a slotted spoon, remove ¼ cup of the cooked rice and reserve. Transfer the carrots, onion, remaining rice and 1 cup of the cooking liquid to a blender or a food processor and puree until smooth. Return the puree to the soup pot.

4. Mix in the evaporated skimmed milk, salt, pepper, nutmeg and reserved ¼ cup cooked rice. Simmer 5 minutes longer.

Calories: 179	Protein: 5 gm	Total Fat: 7 gm
Saturated Fat: 1 gm	Cholesterol: 1 mg	Carbohydrates: 24 gm
Sodium: 518 mg	Dietary Fiber: 2 gm	

A SUPER SOURCE OF:

Vitamin A ━━━━━━━━━━━━━━━━━━━━━━━━━━ 100%

0%   U.S. Recommended Daily Allowance   100%

*S*tir-Fried Chicken with Rice and Peanuts

Inspired by Chinese cooking, this easy stir-fry dish is seasoned with soy and ginger and made crunchy with broccoli, carrots and peanuts. 5 SERVINGS

2 tablespoons corn oil
2 cups broccoli florets
1 cup sliced carrots
¼ cup sliced scallions
2 garlic cloves, minced
1 pound skinless boneless chicken breasts, cut into 1-inch
  chunks
2 tablespoons reduced-sodium soy sauce
2 tablespoons dry sherry
1 teaspoon grated fresh ginger
2 cups chicken stock or canned low-sodium broth
1 cup long-grain white rice
¼ cup chopped peanuts

1. In a wok or large skillet, heat 1 tablespoon of the oil over medium heat. Add the broccoli, carrots, scallions and garlic and stir-fry until crisp-tender, 3 to 5 minutes. Remove the vegetables from the pan with a slotted spoon and reserve.

2. Heat the remaining 1 tablespoon oil in the wok. Add the chicken and stir-fry until white throughout but still moist, about 5 minutes. Add the soy sauce, sherry and ginger. Cook, stirring, 2 minutes. With a slotted spoon, remove the chicken from the pan and set aside.

3. Add the chicken stock to the wok and heat to boiling over high heat. Add the rice. Reduce the heat to simmer and cook, covered, until the rice is tender, about 18 to 20 minutes. Stir in the chicken, vegetables and peanuts. Remove from the heat. Let stand, covered, 5 minutes.

Calories: 371	Protein: 29 gm	Total Fat: 11 gm
Saturated Fat: 2 gm	Cholesterol: 53 mg	Carbohydrates: 38 gm
Sodium: 343 mg	Dietary Fiber: 2 gm	

A SUPER SOURCE OF:

Phosphorus	27%
Vitamin A	100%
Thiamin	21%
Niacin	70%
Vitamin C	72%

0%   U.S. Recommended Daily Allowance   100%

*T*una-Rice Salad with Jicama

Jicama (pronounced "HICK-a-ma") is a root vegetable from Mexico with a mild flavor and crisp texture similar to a fresh Chinese water chestnut. In this country, jicama is used chiefly in salads; in Mexico, much of it is eaten as a snack—peeled, thinly sliced and seasoned with lime juice, salt and ground red pepper.

5 SERVINGS

1 cup long-grain white rice
1 large can (14 ounces) water-packed white tuna, drained and flaked
2 celery stalks, sliced
1 green bell pepper, chopped
1 red bell pepper, chopped
½ cup diced peeled jicama
¼ cup chopped parsley
½ cup nonfat plain yogurt
2 tablespoons safflower oil
1 tablespoon fresh lemon juice
2 scallions, minced
½ teaspoon salt
¼ teaspoon white pepper
2 teaspoons capers

1. In a medium saucepan, heat 2 cups water to boiling over high heat. Add the rice. Reduce the heat to a simmer, cover and cook until the rice is tender, 18 to 20 minutes. Drain and let cool.

2. Place the rice in a large bowl. Add the tuna, celery, green and red bell peppers, jicama and parsley. Toss to mix.

3. In a small bowl, prepare a dressing by whisking together the yogurt, oil, lemon juice, scallions, salt and white pepper. Add the capers. Spoon the dressing over the salad and toss to coat.

Calories: 315	Protein: 24 gm	Total Fat: 8 gm
Saturated Fat: 1 gm	Cholesterol: 31 mg	Carbohydrates: 35 gm
Sodium: 574 mg	Dietary Fiber: 2 gm	

A SUPER SOURCE OF:

Vitamin A	━━━━━ 28%	
Niacin	━━━━━ 31%	
Vitamin C	━━━━━━━━━━━━━ 96%	

0%   U.S. Recommended Daily Allowance   100%

*S*tuffed Peppers

6 SERVINGS

6 large green bell peppers
1 tablespoon safflower oil
1 medium onion, chopped
1 garlic clove, minced
½ pound turkey sausage
1 cup long-grain white rice
1 cup crushed tomatoes, with their juice
1½ cups chicken stock or canned low-sodium broth
2 tablespoons chopped fresh basil
2 tablespoons chopped fresh parsley
¼ teaspoon ground pepper
¼ cup grated Parmesan cheese

1. Preheat the oven to 350 degrees. Lightly coat a 9-inch square baking dish with vegetable cooking spray. Cut a thin slice from the top of each pepper and remove the core.

2. In a medium skillet, heat the oil over medium heat. Add the onion and garlic and cook until soft but not brown, about 5 minutes. Add the turkey sausage and cook, stirring and breaking up the meat with a wooden spoon, until browned and cooked through, about 7 minutes.

3. Add the rice and stir to coat. Pour in the tomatoes with their juice and the stock. Add the basil, parsley and pepper. Reduce the heat to a simmer, cover and cook until the rice is tender, about 18 minutes.

4. Lightly pack each pepper with the cooked turkey-rice mixture. Place the peppers into the prepared pan. Spoon any extra filling into the pan around the peppers. Sprinkle the grated cheese over the peppers. Bake 20 minutes, or until the peppers can be easily pierced with the tip of a knife but still hold their shape and the tops are golden and crusty.

Calories: 259	Protein: 12 gm	Total Fat: 9 gm
Saturated Fat: 3 gm	Cholesterol: 26 mg	Carbohydrates: 34 gm
Sodium: 280 mg	Dietary Fiber: 2 gm	

A SUPER SOURCE OF:

Iron	21%
Thiamin	20%
Riboflavin	54%
Niacin	20%
Vitamin C	100%

0%   U.S. Recommended Daily Allowance   100%

*R*ice Pudding

This pudding's so rich and creamy, it's hard to believe it's made with skim milk. 6 SERVINGS

⅓ cup raisins
1 quart skim milk
½ cup long-grain white rice (not converted)
⅓ cup sugar
1 tablespoon vanilla extract
1 whole egg
2 egg whites
1 tablespoon cinnamon

1. In a small bowl, place the raisins and ½ cup warm water. Let stand for 30 minutes to plump. Drain well.

2. In a medium saucepan, heat 3 cups of the skim milk to boiling over medium heat. Add the rice. Reduce the heat to a simmer, cover and cook for 45 minutes.

3. In a medium bowl, blend the sugar, vanilla extract, whole egg, egg whites and remaining 1 cup milk. Add the drained raisins.

4. Stir ½ cup of the hot milk and rice into the egg mixture. Stir the egg mixture back into the pot. Heat over low heat; do not boil.

5. Pour the hot rice into a baking pan. Sprinkle with the cinnamon. Refrigerate the pudding for several hours until cold.

Calories: 208	Protein: 9 gm	Total Fat: 1 gm
Saturated Fat: 0 gm	Cholesterol: 39 mg	Carbohydrates: 39 gm
Sodium: 116 mg	Dietary Fiber: 1 gm	

A SUPER SOURCE OF:

Calcium	23%
Phosphorus	21%

0%   U.S. Recommended Daily Allowance   100%

Rice is an excellent grain for people allergic to wheat or on a gluten-free diet. Rice flour can be substituted for wheat flour in many recipes, and granulated rice, often called "Cream of Rice," can be used in pancakes and muffins and to bread chicken, fish, cutlets and croquettes.

Smoked Turkey Risotto

Risotto is a Northern Italian dish that turns out best if made with Arborio rice imported from Italy. The dish is perfect when the rice grains are separate, tender yet firm, and surrounded by a rich creamy sauce. Medium-low heat and careful stirring are the secrets to the success of this festive dish. 4 SERVINGS

1 tablespoon unsalted butter
3 scallions, chopped
1 medium red bell pepper, chopped
½ green bell pepper, chopped
¾ cup Arborio rice
½ pound smoked turkey breast, cut into ½-inch dice
½ teaspoon salt
¼ teaspoon pepper
¼ cup dry white wine
About 2½ cups chicken stock or canned low-sodium broth
¼ cup grated Parmesan cheese

1. In a medium saucepan, melt the butter over medium heat. Add the scallions and bell peppers. Cook until the peppers are softened, about 5 minutes.

2. Add the rice and stir to coat. Cook, stirring, until translucent, 1 to 2 minutes. Add the smoked turkey, salt and pepper.

3. Pour in the wine and ½ cup of the chicken stock. Cook over medium-low heat, stirring frequently, until most of the liquid is absorbed. Continue adding stock ½ cup at a time, cooking and stirring until the rice is just tender and the sauce has a creamy consistency.

4. Stir in the cheese. Mix to combine. Serve immediately.

Calories: 261	Protein: 18	Total Fat: 7 gm
Saturated Fat: 3 gm	Cholesterol: 29 mg	Carbohydrates: 31 gm
Sodium: 893 mg	Dietary Fiber: 1 gm	

A SUPER SOURCE OF:

Phosphorus	26%
Vitamin A	36%
Niacin	37%
Vitamin C	87%

0%   U.S. Recommended Daily Allowance   100%

Rice is an excellent source of complex carbohydrates, with 131 calories per ½-cup serving of cooked white rice. Brown rice has an even lower caloric content: 109 calories per ½-cup serving.

Arroz Con Pollo

Arroz Con Pollo is Spanish for "Rice with Chicken." There are countless variations of this classic dish. Here is one tasty interpretation. 6 SERVINGS

2 garlic cloves, crushed
1½ teaspoons oregano
2 teaspoons cumin
½ teaspoon salt
¼ teaspoon pepper
1 tablespoon olive oil, preferably extra virgin
1 teaspoon red wine vinegar
1½ pounds chicken thighs, skin removed
1 medium onion, chopped
1 medium red bell pepper, chopped
1 carrot, chopped
¼ to ½ teaspoon crushed hot pepper flakes
½ pound turkey sausage
1 cup long-grain white rice
2 cups canned crushed tomatoes, with their juice
2 cups chicken stock or canned low-sodium broth
¼ cup chopped pitted green or black olives
2 teaspoons capers
1 cup fresh or frozen peas

1. Preheat the oven to 350 degrees. In a small bowl, mash the garlic, oregano, cumin, salt and pepper to a paste. Stir in 1 teaspoon of the olive oil and the vinegar. Rub the mixture over the chicken pieces. Place the chicken in a roasting pan large enough to hold the pieces in a single layer. Bake 50 to 55 minutes, or until the chicken is tender and the juices run clear.

2. In a large nonstick skillet, heat the remaining 2 teaspoons oil over medium heat. Add the onion, bell pepper, carrot and hot pepper flakes. Cook until the onion is soft but not brown, about 5 minutes. Add the turkey sausage and cook, stirring and breaking up the meat with a wooden spoon, until the meat is browned and cooked through, about 7 minutes.

3. **A**dd the rice and stir to coat. Pour in the tomatoes with their juice and the stock. Reduce the heat to a simmer, cover and cook until the rice is tender and the liquid is absorbed, 18 to 20 minutes. Place the olives, capers, peas and baked chicken over the rice in the pan. Cook, covered, 5 minutes longer.

Calories: 326	Protein: 24 gm	Total Fat: 9 gm
Saturated Fat: 3 gm	Cholesterol: 61 mg	Carbohydrates: 36 gm
Sodium: 735 mg	Dietary Fiber: 3 gm	

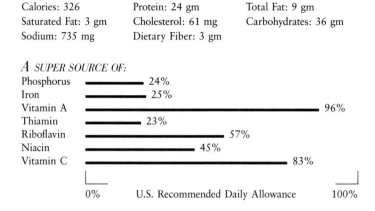

A SUPER SOURCE OF:

Phosphorus	24%
Iron	25%
Vitamin A	96%
Thiamin	23%
Riboflavin	57%
Niacin	45%
Vitamin C	83%

0%   U.S. Recommended Daily Allowance   100%

To reheat cooked rice in a microwave oven, put rice in a micro-waveproof baking dish and cook on High about 1½ minutes per 1 cup of cooked rice.

To reheat cooked rice, put rice in a saucepan with a tight-fitting lid and add 2 tablespoons water for each 1 cup of cooked rice. Cook 4 to 5 minutes over low heat.

*R*isotto *Verde*

Risotto is a northern Italian dish in which rice is cooked in a unique way. The uncooked grain is sautéed briefly in fat, then hot liquid is added a bit at a time while the pot is stirred constantly. The risotto is ready when the rice is creamy but still firm to the bite—al dente, as the Italians say. 4 SERVINGS

3 small zucchini
1 tablespoon olive oil, preferably extra virgin
3 scallions, chopped
1 garlic clove, minced
³/₄ cup Arborio rice
¹/₂ teaspoon salt
¹/₄ teaspoon pepper
¹/₄ cup dry white wine
About 2¹/₂ cups chicken stock or canned low-sodium broth
¹/₄ cup grated Parmesan cheese
¹/₂ cup chopped fresh cilantro or parsley

1. Shred the zucchini. Squeeze out all the moisture by wringing in a double thickness of paper towel or cheesecloth.

2. In a medium saucepan, heat the olive oil over medium-high heat. Add the zucchini, scallions and garlic and cook, stirring occasionally, until soft and most of the liquid has evaporated, about 5 minutes.

3. Add the rice and stir to coat. Cook, stirring, until translucent, 1 to 2 minutes. Add the salt and pepper.

4. Pour in the wine and ¹/₂ cup of the stock. Cook over medium-low heat, stirring frequently, until most of the liquid is absorbed. Continue adding stock, ¹/₂ cup at a time, stirring, until the rice is barely tender and the sauce is creamy in consistency.

5. Stir in the cheese and cilantro. Mix to combine. Serve immediately.

Calories: 215	Protein: 7 gm	Total Fat: 6 gm
Saturated Fat: 2 gm	Cholesterol: 4 mg	Carbohydrates: 32 gm
Sodium: 406 mg	Dietary Fiber: 1 gm	

Like other cultivated plants, rice is highly variable. Mature plants can grow from 1 to 6 feet tall, and the chaff surrounding the grain can be yellow, white, red or black.

*R*isotto with Fresh Peas

This Italian favorite, known as *"risi e bisi"* in the old country, can be served as a side dish or as a separate course. To lower fat content, smoked turkey has been substituted for the pancetta (Italian bacon) or prosciutto usually called for. 4 SERVINGS

2 teaspoons unsalted butter
2 teaspoons olive oil
1 medium onion, chopped
1 celery stalk, chopped
3/4 cup Arborio rice
1/4 teaspoon pepper
2 1/2 cups chicken stock or canned low-sodium broth
1/4 cup dry white wine
1 cup shelled fresh or frozen peas
1/2 cup boiling water
2 ounces smoked turkey breast, cut into 1/2-inch dice
1/4 cup grated Parmesan cheese

1. In a medium saucepan, melt the butter in the olive oil over medium heat. Add the onion and celery and cook until soft but not brown, 3 to 5 minutes.

2. Add the rice and stir to coat. Cook, stirring, until translucent, 1 to 2 minutes. Add the pepper.

3. Pour in the stock and wine and bring to a boil. Reduce the heat to a simmer, cover and cook until the liquid is absorbed and the rice is just tender, about 20 minutes.

4. In a small saucepan, cook the fresh peas in the boiling water until they are just tender, about 5 minutes. Drain.

5. Add the peas, smoked turkey and Parmesan cheese to the cooked rice. Stir gently to combine. Serve immediately.

Calories: 260	Protein: 11 gm	Total Fat: 7 gm
Saturated Fat: 3 gm	Cholesterol: 14 mg	Carbohydrates: 37 gm
Sodium: 262 mg	Dietary Fiber: 2 gm	

A SUPER SOURCE OF:

Thiamin	▬▬▬	21%
Niacin	▬▬▬	22%
Vitamin C	▬▬▬▬	30%

0%   U.S. Recommended Daily Allowance   100%

Salmon and Texmati Rice Salad

Although pink salmon can be used, canned red salmon will give this salad the best flavor and appearance. Either way, the salmon is an excellent source of protein and cholesterol-lowering Omega-2 oil. 5 SERVINGS

2 cups Basmati rice
1/4 cup fresh lime juice
2 tablespoons canola or safflower oil
2 tablespoons Asian sesame oil
2 tablespoons reduced-sodium soy sauce
1 garlic clove, minced
1 tablespoon minced fresh dill or 1 teaspoon dried
3 scallions, chopped
1 celery stalk, chopped
1 yellow or red bell pepper, chopped
1 large can (15½ ounces) red Sockeye salmon, drained and broken into chunks

1. In a medium saucepan, heat 4 cups water to boiling over high heat. Add the rice. Reduce the heat to a simmer, cover and cook until the rice is tender, about 25 minutes. Drain and let cool.

2. In a small bowl, prepare a dressing by whisking the lime juice, canola oil, sesame oil, soy sauce, garlic and dill, or by shaking the ingredients together in a jar with a tight-fitting lid.

3. In a large salad bowl, combine the cooled cooked rice with the scallions, celery, bell pepper and salmon. Pour the dressing over the salad and toss to coat.

Calories: 492	Protein: 21 gm	Total Fat: 17 gm
Saturated Fat: 2 gm	Cholesterol: 31 mg	Carbohydrates: 63 gm
Sodium: 637 mg	Dietary Fiber: 1 gm	

A SUPER SOURCE OF:

Calcium	21%
Phosphorus	34%
Iron	25%
Vitamin A	29%
Thiamin	29%
Niacin	37%
Vitamin C	61%

0%   U.S. Recommended Daily Allowance   100%

Curried Cod on a Bed of Basmati Rice

4 SERVINGS

1 cup Basmati rice
1 garlic clove, minced
1 tablespoon curry powder
½ teaspoon cumin
½ teaspoon chili powder
¼ cup fresh lemon juice
1 pound fresh cod fillets, cut into 4 pieces
1 tablespoon safflower oil
1 medium onion, chopped
1 cup plus 3 tablespoons dry white wine
1 tablespoon cornstarch
¼ cup golden raisins
¼ cup chopped almonds

1. Soak the rice several times in cold water, draining between each soaking, until the water is clear. Soak again and let stand for 30 minutes; drain. In a large saucepan of boiling water, cook the rice for 5 minutes; drain.

2. In a small bowl, combine the garlic, curry powder, cumin, chili powder and lemon juice. Brush over the cod to coat and marinate in the refrigerator for 1 hour.

3. In a large skillet, heat the oil over medium heat. Add the onion and cook until soft but not brown, about 5 minutes. Add 1 cup of the wine and cook 2 minutes to reduce slightly. In a small bowl, blend the cornstarch with the remaining 3 tablespoons wine. Stir into the skillet and bring to a boil, stirring until the sauce thickens, about 2 minutes. Reduce the heat to low.

4. Add the raisins and nuts. Carefully add the fish to the skillet. Cover and cook 15 minutes, or until opaque to the center. Mound the rice on a large serving platter. Arrange the fish on top and pour the pan juices over the fish.

Calories: 406	Protein: 26 gm	Total Fat: 9 gm
Saturated Fat: 1 gm	Cholesterol: 49 mg	Carbohydrates: 55 gm
Sodium: 72	Dietary Fiber: 2 gm	

A SUPER SOURCE OF:

Phosphorus	━━━━━━━	36%
Iron	━━━━	22%
Thiamin	━━━━━	26%
Niacin	━━━━	24%

0%   U.S. Recommended Daily Allowance   100%

Ground Turkey and Confetti Brown Rice

Tiny bits of colored vegetables give this one-dish meal a festive air. 6 SERVINGS

1½ cups chicken stock or canned low-sodium broth
1 cup brown rice
2 teaspoons safflower oil
2 scallions, chopped
1 carrot, chopped
½ green bell pepper, finely diced
½ red bell pepper, finely diced
½ yellow bell pepper, finely diced
1 pound lean ground turkey
½ teaspoon salt
¼ teaspoon pepper

1. In a medium saucepan, heat the stock and 1 cup water to boiling over high heat. Add the brown rice. Reduce the heat to a simmer, cover and cook until the rice is tender, about 45 minutes.

2. In a large skillet, heat the oil over medium heat. Add the scallions, carrot and bell peppers and cook, stirring occasionally, until softened, 6 to 8 minutes.

3. Add the ground turkey, salt and pepper. Cook over medium heat, stirring and breaking up the meat with a wooden spoon, until browned and cooked through, about 7 minutes.

4. Stir in the cooked brown rice. Cook until the rice is hot, 3 to 5 minutes.

Calories: 254	Protein: 17 gm	Total Fat: 8 gm
Saturated Fat: 2 gm	Cholesterol: 55 mg	Carbohydrates: 27 gm
Sodium: 274 mg	Dietary Fiber: 2 gm	

A SUPER SOURCE OF:

Phosphorus ▬▬▬ 23%
Vitamin A ▬▬▬▬▬▬▬▬▬ 81%
Niacin ▬▬▬ 24%
Vitamin C ▬▬▬▬▬▬ 51%

0%   U.S. Recommended Daily Allowance   100%

Brown rice has about five times as much fiber as white rice. A ½-cup serving of cooked brown rice provides 1½ grams of dietary fiber; the same-size serving of white rice has four tenths of a gram.

Turkey Tofu Chili with Brown Rice

Tofu has the amazing ability to take on the flavors of the other more assertive ingredients in a recipe. In this version of chili, tofu is combined with ground turkey, chili powder, cumin and oregano for a satisfying meal in a bowl. 6 SERVINGS

1 cup brown rice
2 tablespoons safflower oil
1 large onion, chopped
2 garlic cloves, minced
1 pound very lean ground turkey
1 can (28 ounces) crushed tomatoes, with their juice
1 tablespoon Dijon mustard
2 teaspoons chili powder
1 teaspoon cumin
1 teaspoon oregano
¼ teaspoon pepper
1 cup canned pinto beans, rinsed and drained
1 brick (4 ounces) firm tofu, cut into ½-inch dice

1. In a medium saucepan, heat 2½ cups water to boiling over high heat. Add the brown rice. Reduce the heat to a simmer, cover and cook until the rice is tender, about 45 minutes. Drain and reserve.

2. In a large skillet, heat the oil over medium heat. Add the onion and garlic and cook until soft but not brown, about 5 minutes. Add the turkey and cook, stirring and breaking up the meat with a spoon, until browned and cooked through, about 7 minutes.

3. Add the tomatoes with their juice. Reduce the heat to low. Add the mustard, chili powder, cumin, oregano and pepper. Stir well to blend. Cover and cook until the flavors combine and some of the liquid has evaporated, about 40 minutes.

4. Add the pinto beans and tofu. Mix in lightly and simmer 15 minutes longer. For each serving, place about ½ cup of the cooked brown rice in a deep soup bowl. Spoon the chili over the rice.

Calories: 364	Protein: 22 gm	Total Fat: 14 gm
Saturated Fat: 2 gm	Cholesterol: 55 mg	Carbohydrates: 39 gm
Sodium: 463 mg	Dietary Fiber: 4 gm	

A SUPER SOURCE OF:

Phosphorus	33%
Iron	29%
Vitamin A	23%
Thiamin	20%
Niacin	27%
Vitamin C	39%

0%   U.S. Recommended Daily Allowance   100%

Turkey and Brown Rice Salad with Beans and Salsa

5 SERVINGS

2½ cups chicken stock or canned low-sodium broth
1 cup brown rice
1 tablespoon safflower oil
1 medium onion, chopped
1 medium green bell pepper, chopped
1 garlic clove, minced
1½ cups canned crushed tomatoes, with their juice
¾ pound cooked turkey breast, cut into ½-inch cubes
1 cup canned kidney beans, rinsed and drained
1 medium tomato, chopped
3 scallions, chopped
¼ cup chopped fresh cilantro or parsley
2 tablespoons fresh lemon juice
1 teaspoon cumin
¼ teaspoon crushed hot pepper flakes
3 drops of Worcestershire sauce

1. In a medium saucepan, heat the stock to boiling over high heat. Add the brown rice. Reduce the heat to a simmer, cover and cook until the rice is tender, 40 to 45 minutes. Drain and let cool.

2. In a medium skillet, heat the oil over medium heat. Add the onion, bell pepper and garlic and cook until soft but not brown, about 5 minutes.

3. Add the tomatoes with their juice, turkey and kidney beans. Cook over medium heat, stirring occasionally, 15 minutes, or until slightly reduced. Stir in the chopped tomato, scallions, cilantro, lemon juice, cumin, hot pepper flakes and Worcestershire sauce. Cook 5 minutes longer.

4. Place the rice in a large bowl. Add the hot turkey mixture and toss until evenly combined. Serve at room temperature.

Calories: 352	Protein: 27 gm	Total Fat: 7 gm
Saturated Fat: 1 gm	Cholesterol: 47 mg	Carbohydrates: 44 gm
Sodium: 319 mg	Dietary Fiber: 6 gm	

A SUPER SOURCE OF:

Phosphorus	━━━━━━ 31%
Vitamin A	━━━━━ 26%
Niacin	━━━━━━━ 39%
Vitamin C	━━━━━━━━━━━━━ 71%

0%	U.S. Recommended Daily Allowance	100%

Lamb, Brown Rice and Sautéed Spinach Salad

6 SERVINGS

2½ cups beef stock or canned low-sodium beef broth
1 cup brown rice
¼ cup safflower oil
¼ pound mushrooms, sliced
2 shallots, chopped
1 pound fresh spinach leaves, washed well and drained, or
   1 box (10 ounces) frozen spinach, thawed and drained
1 pound cooked lean lamb, cut into ½-inch chunks
¼ cup raisins
¼ cup pine nuts
3 tablespoons fresh lemon juice
1 garlic clove, minced
1 teaspoon curry powder
½ teaspoon cumin
½ teaspoon salt
¼ teaspoon pepper
¼ teaspoon nutmeg

1. In a medium saucepan, heat the stock to boiling over high heat. Add the brown rice, reduce the heat, cover and simmer until the rice is tender, about 45 minutes; drain.

2. In a large skillet, heat 1 tablespoon of the oil over medium heat. Add the mushrooms and shallots and cook until tender, about 5 minutes. Add the spinach and cook until it is wilted and the liquid evaporates, 3 to 5 minutes.

3. In a large bowl, place the rice, lamb and cooked vegetables. Add the raisins and pine nuts.

4. In a small bowl, whisk together the lemon juice, garlic, curry powder, cumin, salt, pepper, nutmeg and the remaining 3 tablespoons oil. Pour the dressing over the salad and toss to coat.

Calories: 432	Protein: 27 gm	Total Fat: 21 gm
Saturated Fat: 4 gm	Cholesterol: 66 mg	Carbohydrates: 36 gm
Sodium: 299 mg	Dietary Fiber: 4 gm	

A SUPER SOURCE OF:

Iron	31%
Vitamin B12	27%
Vitamin A	100%
Niacin	41%
Vitamin C	43%
Zinc	30%

0%   U.S. Recommended Daily Allowance   100%

Chicken Stuffed with Broccoli and Brown Rice

A vegetable-rice stuffing is inserted under the skin of the chicken, keeping it very moist as it roasts. Discard the skin after baking to reduce the fat and calorie content. 6 SERVINGS

½ cup brown rice
2 teaspoons safflower oil
1 medium onion, chopped
¼ pound mushrooms, chopped
1 garlic clove, minced
½ pound fresh or frozen broccoli, chopped, cooked and
   well drained
1¼ cups chicken stock or canned low-sodium broth
½ teaspoon cinnamon
¼ teaspoon ginger
½ teaspoon salt
¼ teaspoon pepper
6 small chicken breasts (3½ to 4 ounces each)
4 scallions, chopped
2 carrots, chopped
1 tablespoon honey
1 cup dry white wine
1 tablespoon cornstarch

1. In a medium saucepan, heat 1¼ cups water to boiling over high heat. Add the rice. Reduce the heat to a simmer, cover and cook until the rice is tender, 45 minutes; drain.

2. Preheat the oven to 375 degrees. In a large nonstick skillet, heat the oil over medium-high heat. Add the onion, mushrooms and garlic and cook until soft and most of the liquid has evaporated, 6 to 8 minutes.

3. In a large bowl, combine the onion-mushroom mixture, cooked brown rice, broccoli, ¼ cup of stock, cinnamon, ginger, salt and pepper. Mix well.

4. Carefully separate the skin of the chicken from the meat without tearing the skin; leave it attached where possible. Evenly divide the stuffing and spread it between the skin and the meat. Close the opening with toothpicks or small metal skewers.

5. In a baking pan large enough to hold the chicken in a single layer, put the scallions and carrots. Place the chicken over the vegetables. In a medium bowl, combine the remaining cup of stock with the honey and wine. Stir to blend. Pour around the chicken. Bake 1 hour, or until the juices run clear, basting occasionally with the liquid in the pan.

6. Transfer the chicken to a serving platter and cover with foil to keep warm. Strain the pan juices into a small saucepan. Heat until hot. In a small bowl, blend the cornstarch with 2 tablespoons cold water. Add to the juices and bring to a boil, stirring until thickened. Pour the sauce over the chicken.

Calories: 258	Protein: 26 gm	Total Fat: 6 gm
Saturated Fat: 1 gm	Cholesterol: 60 mg	Carbohydrates: 24 gm
Sodium: 281 mg	Dietary Fiber: 3 gm	

A SUPER SOURCE OF:

Phosphorus	31%
Vitamin A	100%
Niacin	65%
Vitamin C	75%

0%   U.S. Recommended Daily Allowance   100%

Parboiled rice can be substituted for regular long-grain rice in many recipes by slightly increasing liquids and adding about 5 minutes to the cooking time.

Storing cooked rice is easy. Make sure the container is airtight so the kernels don't dry out, then keep in the refrigerator for up to 1 week or the freezer for up to 6 months.

*A*pricot and Pecan Brown Rice

4 SERVINGS

¼ *cup coarsely chopped pecans*
2½ *cups chicken stock or canned low-sodium broth*
1 *cup brown rice*
¼ *cup coarsely chopped dried apricots*
½ *teaspoon salt*
¼ *teaspoon pepper*
2 *tablespoons fresh lemon juice*
2 *tablespoons safflower oil*
2 *celery stalks, chopped*
4 *scallions, chopped*
¼ *cup chopped parsley*
⅓ *cup nonfat plain yogurt*
1 *tablespoon Dijon mustard*

1. Preheat the oven to 325 degrees. Place the pecans on a small baking sheet. Bake until barely toasted, 6 to 8 minutes. Remove the nuts from the pan and cool completely on a paper towel. In a food processor fitted with the metal blade, or with a sharp knife, coarsely chop the pecans.

2. Increase the oven temperature to 375 degrees. Lightly coat a 2-quart baking dish with vegetable cooking spray.

3. In a medium saucepan, heat the chicken stock over high heat to boiling. Add the brown rice, apricots and salt. Reduce the heat to low, cover and cook until the rice is tender, about 45 minutes.

4. In a large bowl, combine the rice mixture with the pepper, lemon juice, oil, celery, scallions, parsley, yogurt and mustard. Mix well. Stir in the toasted pecans.

5. Spoon the rice mixture into the prepared pan. Cover with a lid or aluminum foil and bake for 15 minutes. Uncover and bake 15 minutes longer, or until slightly crispy on top.

Calories: 340	Protein: 7 gm	Total Fat: 14 gm
Saturated Fat: 2 gm	Cholesterol: 0 mg	Carbohydrates: 47 gm
Sodium: 457 mg	Dietary Fiber: 4 gm	

A SUPER SOURCE OF:

Phosphorus	━━━━━━	23%
Vitamin A	━━━━━━━━	31%
Vitamin C	━━━━━━━	26%

0%   U.S. Recommended Daily Allowance   100%

*W*ild Rice and Turkey Salad

Wild rice doesn't come cheap, but its flavor is worth the price, especially when you want to wow special guests or mark a very special occasion. 6 SERVINGS

3 cups chicken stock or canned low-sodium broth
1 cup wild rice
1 pound cooked turkey breast, cut into 1-inch cubes
2 tart cooking apples, such as Granny Smith, peeled and
  cut into 1/2-inch cubes
1 medium red bell pepper, chopped
1/4 cup raisins
2 tablespoons chopped pecans
1/4 cup olive oil
1/4 cup balsamic vinegar
2 shallots, chopped
2 tablespoons chopped parsley
1/2 teaspoon salt
1/4 teaspoon pepper

1. In a medium saucepan, heat the stock to boiling over high heat. Add the wild rice. Reduce the heat to a simmer, cover and cook until the rice is tender, 45 to 50 minutes. Drain and let cool.

2. In a large salad bowl, combine the wild rice, turkey, apples, bell pepper, raisins and pecans. Toss to mix.

3. In a small bowl, prepare a dressing by whisking together the olive oil, vinegar, shallots, parsley, salt and pepper, or by shaking the ingredients together in a jar with a tight-fitting lid. Pour the dressing over the salad and toss until evenly combined.

Calories: 371   Protein: 28 gm   Total Fat: 14 gm
Saturated Fat: 2 gm   Cholesterol: 52 mg   Carbohydrates: 34 gm
Sodium: 264 mg   Dietary Fiber: 3 gm

A SUPER SOURCE OF:

Phosphorus ━━━━━━━━ 30%
Niacin   ━━━━━━━━━ 38%
Vitamin C   ━━━━━━━━━━ 45%
Zinc   ━━━━━ 22%

0%   U.S. Recommended Daily Allowance   100%

A BRAN BONANZA

"Bran" is the name for the outer protective layers that surround the kernels of grains, and for years the word meant little to Americans. It had something to do with wheat, and it was an ingredient in muffins and ready-to-eat breakfast cereals. Then something happened.

In March 1988, the American Medical Association released a study suggesting that a diet high in fiber, including oat bran, might help to reduce blood cholesterol in some individuals. The media picked up on the report, trumpeted it across the nation and, within weeks, a new food fad was off and running. Oat bran was hailed as a miracle food; rice bran wasn't far behind. Ordinary folk began sprinkling the stuff over everything from soup to nuts. Commercial bakers scrambled to put it into all kinds of things, particularly muffins.

What made this all a fad at first, and not an important diet trend, was that too many people continued consuming unhealthy quantities of the butter, lard and other hard fats in the belief they now had oat and rice brans to protect their arteries from any amount of excess. Too often the baked products contained lots of solid shortening and only a pinch of bran.

Unfortunately for those seeking easy solutions, magic isn't one of bran's strong points. It is, however, wonderfully nutritious stuff, whether it's from wheat, oats or rice. Besides protein, vitamins and minerals, wheat bran is full of the kind of fiber that's good for digestive health. And there's evidence indicating that the soluble fiber in oat bran and the oil in rice bran can help reduce cholesterol in the blood.

▲ **Wheat bran,** like wheat germ, is a by-product of the milling of white flour. The wheat kernels are broken up, and the bran and germ are separated from the starchy endosperm by sifting or "bolting" through fine-meshed fabric. The several bran layers represent about 13 percent of the total weight of a wheat berry.

▲ **Rice bran** is a by-product of the milling of white rice. Rice is naturally "brown" or tawny, the grains covered with bran that is milled or "polished" away to produce white rice.

▲ **Oat bran** is a special case, since most oat products—rolled oats, steel-cut oats and so on—are normally made with the whole grain. However, whole or rolled oats can be ground into a coarse flour and the bran separated by sifting or bolting.

Health food enthusiasts mix bran into casseroles, yogurt and beverages and even use it as a topping for ice cream. But for most of us, bran will likely remain a nutritious addition to things like meat loaf, baked goods, breakfast cereals and breading mixtures for fried foods. Oat bran gives special goodness, texture and flavor to our Banana–Oat Bran Waffles and Fresh Peach Bran Muffins. Raisin–Rice Bran Muffins get their spunk from rice bran, as does Salmon–Rice Bran Cakes with Horseradish Sauce.

Actually, a little nutritional boost can be given to just about any favorite bread, muffin or pancake recipe by substituting oat, rice or wheat bran for some of the flour in the mixture. From each 1 cup of flour remove 2 to 3 tablespoons and replace it with the same amount of bran. This amount shouldn't alter baking characteristics significantly. Adding greater amounts of bran usually requires increasing the baking powder in the recipe or, in the case of yeast breads, tolerating a heavier, denser loaf.

Unlike wheat germ and most whole-grain flours and meal, bran will keep for months at room temperature as long as it's in an airtight container.

Dietary fiber content of brans varies considerably in both amount and type. One ounce of oat bran contains about 4 grams of dietary fiber. The same amount of wheat bran contains about 12.5 grams of fiber. One ounce of rice bran contains about 6 grams of fiber.

*H*oney Mustard–Oat Bran–Pecan Chicken

Oat bran, pecans, honey and mustard all combine to make these baked chicken thighs a dish suited for anything from a sit-down dinner to a family picnic. Boneless thighs are used here, but other chicken parts can be substituted. 4 SERVINGS

¼ cup plus 2 tablespoons Dijon mustard
1½ tablespoons honey
¼ cup plus 2 tablespoons orange juice
1 garlic clove, minced
1 teaspoon grated fresh ginger
¼ teaspoon pepper
6 boneless chicken thighs, skin removed
1 cup crushed oat bran flakes
¼ cup finely chopped pecans
¼ cup water

1. **P**reheat the oven to 375 degrees. Lightly coat a 9-inch square baking pan with vegetable cooking spray.

2. **I**n a small bowl, combine the mustard, honey, 2 tablespoons orange juice, garlic, ginger and pepper. With a pastry brush, coat both sides of the chicken with the mixture.

3. **I**n a shallow dish, place the oat bran flakes and pecans. Mix to combine. Pat both sides of the chicken thighs with the crumbs. Place in the prepared pan. Pour the ¼ cup of orange juice and the water around the meat. Bake 45 to 50 minutes, or until the juices run clear and the chicken is crisp and golden brown on top.

Calories: 331	Protein: 24 gm	Total Fat: 11 gm
Saturated Fat: 1 gm	Cholesterol: 86 mg	Carbohydrates: 35 gm
Sodium: 775 mg	Dietary Fiber: 3 gm	

A SUPER SOURCE OF:

Phosphorus	━━━━━━━━	34%
Niacin	━━━━━━━━	35%
Vitamin C	━━━━━	21%
Zinc	━━━━━	20%

0%   U.S. Recommended Daily Allowance   100%

*B*anana–Oat Bran Waffles

Topped with sliced bananas and nonfat vanilla frozen yogurt, these waffles are a healthy dessert, and high in potassium, too.

3 SERVINGS

1 large ripe banana
2 egg whites
1 cup skim milk
3 tablespoons safflower oil
1 cup all-purpose flour
½ cup oat bran
2 tablespoons sugar
2 teaspoons baking powder

1. Lightly coat a waffle iron with vegetable cooking spray and preheat.

2. In a blender or food processor, place the banana, egg whites, milk and oil. Blend until thoroughly combined.

3. In a medium bowl, place the flour, oat bran, sugar and baking powder. Add the banana mixture and stir only until moistened; the batter should be slightly lumpy.

4. Pour ⅓ cup of the batter onto the prepared waffle iron and cook 4 to 5 minutes, or until golden brown and crisp. Repeat with the remaining batter. Serve the waffles immediately with fresh fruit or fruit sauce.

Calories: 427	Protein: 13 gm	Total Fat: 16 gm
Saturated Fat: 2 gm	Cholesterol: 2 mg	Carbohydrates: 65 gm
Sodium: 366 mg	Dietary Fiber: 4 gm	

A SUPER SOURCE OF:

Calcium	━━━━━━ 26%
Phosphorus	━━━━━━ 29%
Thiamin	━━━━━━━ 37%
Riboflavin	━━━━━━ 28%

0%   U.S. Recommended Daily Allowance   100%

A 1-ounce serving (⅓ cup) of plain oat bran provides 70 calories from 19 grams of carbohydrates, 5 grams of protein and 2 grams of fat. Many oat bran cereals have other grains added, which changes the nutritional profile.

*F*resh Peach Bran Muffins

Ripe and juicy summer peaches taste wonderful unadorned. When you want to turn them into a baked treat, a batch of these fresh and fruity muffins is the perfect answer. MAKES 12 MUFFINS

1 cup oat bran
½ cup all-purpose flour
¼ cup whole wheat flour
¼ cup sugar
2 teaspoons baking powder
½ teaspoon baking soda
1½ teaspoons grated orange zest
½ teaspoon nutmeg
½ teaspoon mace
¼ teaspoon salt
1 cup nonfat peach yogurt
¼ cup safflower oil
1 egg
2 medium peaches, peeled and cut into ½-inch dice

1. Preheat the oven to 400 degrees. Line a 12-count muffin tin with paper baking cups.
2. In a large bowl, combine the oat bran, all-purpose flour, whole wheat flour, sugar, baking powder, baking soda, orange zest, nutmeg, mace and salt.
3. In another bowl, place the yogurt, oil and egg. Whisk until well blended. Stir in the peaches. Add all at once to the dry ingredients. Stir only until moistened; the batter should be slightly lumpy.
4. Spoon the batter evenly into the prepared pan. Bake 20 to 25 minutes, or until the muffins are golden and springy to the touch. Remove the muffins from the pan and let cool on a wire rack.

Calories: 137 per muffin   Protein: 4 gm   Total Fat: 6 gm
Saturated Fat: 1 gm   Cholesterol: 18 mg   Carbohydrates: 21 gm
Sodium: 167 mg   Dietary Fiber: 2 gm

*A*pple and Honey Cereal Muffins

Kids might enjoy making these muffins with their favorite breakfast flakes. Low-sugar corn, wheat or all-grain cereals work well. MAKES 12 MUFFINS

1 cup oat bran cereal flakes
½ cup all-purpose flour
⅓ cup whole wheat flour
2 teaspoons baking powder
½ teaspoon baking soda
1 teaspoon cinnamon
¼ teaspoon salt
1 egg
1 cup unsweetened applesauce
½ cup nonfat plain yogurt
¼ cup honey
¼ cup sunflower or safflower oil
1 medium sweet apple, such as Delicious, peeled and cut
  into ¼-inch dice

1. Preheat the oven to 400 degrees. Line a 12-count muffin tin with paper baking cups.

2. In a large bowl, combine the cereal, all-purpose flour, whole wheat flour, baking powder, baking soda, cinnamon and salt.

3. In a medium bowl, place the egg, applesauce, yogurt, honey and oil. Whisk until well blended. Stir in the apple. Add the dry ingredients all at once. Stir only until moistened; the batter should be slightly lumpy.

4. Spoon the batter evenly into the prepared pan. Bake 20 to 25 minutes, or until the muffins are golden and springy to the touch. Remove the muffins from the pan and let cool on a wire rack.

Calories per muffin: 136	Protein: 3 gm	Total Fat: 5 gm
Saturated Fat: 1 gm	Cholesterol: 18 mg	Carbohydrates: 21 gm
Sodium: 165 mg	Dietary Fiber: 2 gm	

Lemon–Oat Bran Muffins

These fiber-rich muffins are light, lemony, luscious and good for you, too. MAKES 12 MUFFINS

1 cup oat bran cereal flakes
½ cup whole wheat flour
½ cup all-purpose flour
⅓ cup packed brown sugar
2 teaspoons grated lemon zest
2 teaspoons baking powder
½ teaspoon baking soda
½ teaspoon cinnamon
¼ teaspoon nutmeg
¼ teaspoon salt
1 cup skim milk
1 tablespoon lemon juice
¼ cup safflower oil
1 egg

1. Preheat the oven to 400 degrees. Line a 12-count muffin tin with paper baking cups.

2. In a large bowl, combine the cereal, whole wheat flour, all-purpose flour, brown sugar, lemon zest, baking powder, baking soda, cinnamon, nutmeg and salt.

3. In another mixing bowl, place the milk, lemon juice, oil and egg. Whisk until well blended. Add all at once to the dry ingredients. Stir only until moistened; the batter should be slightly lumpy.

4. Spoon the batter evenly into the prepared pan. Bake 20 to 25 minutes, or until the muffins are golden and springy to the touch. Remove the muffins from the pan and let cool on a wire rack.

Calories: 130 per muffin	Protein: 3 gm	Total Fat: 5 gm
Saturated Fat: 1 gm	Cholesterol: 18 gm	Carbohydrates: 18 gm
Sodium: 212 mg	Dietary Fiber: 1 gm	

Four-Grain Bran Muffins

Three "natural" grains and a high-protein man-made variety go into this recipe. The "man-made" grain is triticale (pronounced "TRIT-i-cal-ee"), a hybrid produced a few years back when plant breeders crossed wheat and rye. To keep these densely textured muffins from getting tough, be sure to use a light hand when combining the dry and liquid mixtures. MAKES 12 MUFFINS

½ *cup buckwheat flour*
½ *cup triticale flour*
½ *cup all-purpose flour*
½ *cup oat bran*
1 *tablespoon grated orange zest*
2 *teaspoons baking powder*
½ *teaspoon baking soda*
1 *teaspoon cinnamon*
¼ *teaspoon salt*
⅓ *cup honey*
¼ *cup safflower oil*
1¼ *cups buttermilk*
1 *egg*

1. Preheat the oven to 375 degrees. Line a 12-count muffin tin with paper baking cups.

2. In a large bowl, combine the buckwheat flour, triticale flour, all-purpose flour, oat bran, orange zest, baking powder, baking soda, cinnamon and salt.

3. In a medium bowl, place the honey, oil, buttermilk and egg. Whisk until well blended. Add all at once to the dry ingredients. Stir only until moistened; the batter should be slightly lumpy.

4. Spoon the batter evenly into the prepared pan. Bake 20 to 25 minutes, or until the muffins are golden and springy to the touch. Remove the muffins from the pan and let cool on a wire rack.

Calories per muffin: 148	Protein: 4 gm	Total Fat: 6 gm
Saturated Fat: 1 gm	Cholesterol: 19 mg	Carbohydrates: 23 gm
Sodium: 183 mg	Dietary Fiber: 1 gm	

*B*ran *Spice Cookies*

Bran and wheat germ combined with cloves, cinnamon and honey give these small treats a boost of nutrition along with a distinctive flavor. MAKES 28 COOKIES

½ cup whole wheat flour
¼ cup all-purpose flour
¼ cup oat bran
¼ cup wheat germ
1 teaspoon baking powder
1 teaspoon cloves
1 teaspoon cinnamon
¼ teaspoon mace
4 tablespoons unsalted butter, softened
¼ cup honey
1 egg
1 teaspoon vanilla extract

1. Preheat the oven to 350 degrees. Lightly coat a cookie sheet with vegetable cooking spray.

2. In a medium bowl, combine the whole wheat flour, all-purpose flour, oat bran, wheat germ, baking powder, cloves, cinnamon and mace.

3. In another medium bowl, using a hand-held electric mixer or a whisk, cream the butter and honey until light and fluffy, about 3 minutes.

4. Add the egg and vanilla extract and mix until incorporated. Stir in the dry ingredients until just combined.

5. Using 2 tablespoons, drop the batter evenly onto the prepared pan, leaving a 1-inch space between the unbaked cookies. Bake 9 to 11 minutes, or until the cookies are slightly springy to the touch. Remove the cookies from the pan and let cool on a wire rack.

Calories per cookie: 45	Protein: 1 gm	Total Fat: 2 gm
Saturated Fat: 1 gm	Cholesterol: 12 mg	Carbohydrates: 6 gm
Sodium: 18 mg	Dietary Fiber: .5 gm	

Wheat germ is an excellent source of thiamin, Vitamin E, phosphorus and zinc. A 1-ounce portion (about ¼ cup) provides nearly a third of the adult Recommended Daily Allowance of these essential nutrients.

Raisin–Rice Bran Muffins

One of the main ingredients in these muffins is rice bran, which is the outer layer of brown rice. Combined with whole wheat flour, buttermilk and raisins, it makes this a tasty recipe to add to your muffin collection. MAKES 12 MUFFINS

¾ cup rice bran
½ cup whole wheat flour
½ cup all-purpose flour
⅓ cup packed brown sugar
2 teaspoons baking powder
½ teaspoon baking soda
¼ cup raisins
1 teaspoon cinnamon
½ teaspoon nutmeg
¼ teaspoon salt
1 cup buttermilk
¼ cup safflower oil
1 egg

1. Preheat the oven to 400 degrees. Line a 12-count muffin tin with paper baking cups.
2. In a large bowl, combine the rice bran, whole wheat flour, all-purpose flour, brown sugar, baking powder, baking soda, raisins, cinnamon, nutmeg and salt.
3. In another mixing bowl, place the buttermilk, oil and egg. Whisk until well blended. Add all at once to the dry ingredients. Stir only until moistened; the batter should be slightly lumpy.
4. Spoon the batter evenly into the prepared pan. Bake 20 to 25 minutes, or until the muffins are golden and springy to the touch. Remove the muffins from the pan and let cool on a wire rack.

Calories per muffin: 140	Dietary Fiber: 2 gm	Carbohydrates: 20 gm
Calories per muffin: 140	Protein: 3 gm	Total Fat: 6 gm
Saturated Fat: 1 gm	Cholesterol: 18 mg	Carbohydrates: 20 gm
Sodium: 180 mg	Dietary Fiber: 2 gm	

Rice bran is rich in magnesium, Vitamin B6, thiamin, niacin and phosphorus. It is also an excellent source of iron, pantothenic acid (a B vitamin), zinc, copper and protein.

Salmon–Rice Bran Cakes with Horseradish Sauce

6 SERVINGS

½ cup rice bran
½ cup skim milk
1 large can (15½ ounces) red Sockeye salmon, drained and
  broken into chunks
2 egg whites
2 scallions, chopped
½ medium green bell pepper, chopped
½ teaspoon dried dill
¼ teaspoon salt
¼ teaspoon white pepper
½ cup nonfat plain yogurt
1 tablespoon prepared red or white horseradish
1 tablespoon chopped onion
1 teaspoon fresh lemon juice
1 tablespoon safflower oil

1. In a large bowl, combine the rice bran and milk. Let sit 5 minutes. Add the salmon, egg whites, scallions, bell pepper, dill, salt and white pepper. Stir to mix well.

2. Divide the salmon mixture into 6 portions and shape them into patties. Place on a plate. Wrap them in aluminum foil and freeze for 15 minutes.

3. In a small bowl, prepare the sauce by combining the yogurt, horseradish, onion and lemon juice. Mix well.

4. In a large skillet, preferably nonstick, heat the oil over medium-high heat. Add the salmon cakes and cook until golden brown on the bottom, about 5 minutes. Turn and cook until golden on the other side, about 3 to 4 minutes. Serve the salmon cakes with the horseradish sauce.

Calories: 161	Protein: 16 gm	Total Fat: 8 gm
Saturated Fat: 1 gm	Cholesterol: 27 mg	Carbohydrates: 7 gm
Sodium: 457 mg	Dietary Fiber: 2 gm	

A SUPER SOURCE OF:

Calcium	▬▬▬ 22%	
Phosphorus	▬▬▬▬▬ 37%	
Niacin	▬▬▬▬ 28%	

0%   U.S. Recommended Daily Allowance   100%

Whole Wheat Raisin Bran Scones

Scones, a Scottish treat, are slightly sweetened wedges of rich biscuit dough. They are frequently made with cream and served with other small treats at midafternoon tea. Here buttermilk adds the moistness and richness without the fat. MAKES 16 SCONES

1 cup all-purpose flour
½ cup whole wheat flour
½ cup wheat bran cereal
¼ cup plus 1 tablespoon sugar
2 teaspoons baking powder
½ teaspoon baking soda
1 teaspoon cinnamon
½ teaspoon nutmeg
⅛ teaspoon salt
4 tablespoons unsalted butter
1 whole egg
2 egg whites
1 cup plus 2 tablespoons buttermilk
¼ cup raisins

1. Preheat the oven to 425 degrees. Lightly coat a cookie sheet with vegetable cooking spray.

2. In a medium bowl, combine the all-purpose flour, whole wheat flour, bran cereal, ¼ cup sugar, baking powder, baking soda, cinnamon, nutmeg and salt. Cut in the butter with a pastry blender or 2 knives until the mixture is crumbly and has the consistency of coarse meal.

3. In a small bowl, beat the whole egg and egg whites until blended. Add the eggs, 1 cup of buttermilk and the raisins to the flour mixture and mix just until combined.

4. On a lightly floured board, knead the dough gently about 5 times, or until it forms a smooth ball. Divide the dough in half and pat each half into a 6-inch circle about ¾ inch thick. Cut the circle into 8 wedges.

5. Transfer the pastry wedges to the prepared cookie sheet. Lightly brush the tops with the remaining 2 tablespoons buttermilk and sprinkle with the remaining 1 tablespoon sugar. Bake 16 to 18 minutes, or until the scones are lightly browned. Serve warm.

Calories per scone: 107	Protein: 3 gm	Total Fat: 4 gm
Saturated Fat: 1 gm	Cholesterol: 22 mg	Carbohydrates: 16 gm
Sodium: 137 mg	Dietary Fiber: 1 gm	

A 1-ounce serving (approximately ⅓ cup) of rice bran provides 90 calories from 14 grams of carbohydrates, 4 grams of protein and 6 grams of fat.

BARLEY, MILLET AND RYE

Among the cereal grains—the grains produced by grasses—barley, millet and rye are the "poor relations." People say they're nice, then don't eat much of them. That's a shame. These grains are every bit as tasty and nutritious as their more popular "cousins." Moreover, it's just a good idea to eat as varied a diet as possible.

BARLEY

For most of us, the only barley we've ever had has been in a soup bowl. This hearty grain has been used to thicken soups and stews since time immemorial, and our savory Beef and Barley Soup and dill-scented Wild Mushroom and Barley Soup are classics of their kind. But once upon a time and now once again, barley has been seeing more uses than that. Until the 1500s, loaves of barley bread were more common in Europe than loaves made of wheat, and now barley flour and meal are showing up once more in muffins and the like.

Cooked barley has a delectable nutlike flavor and an attractive chewy texture. One drawback has been the grain's cooking time—45 to 50 minutes for the medium "pearled" variety—but at least one miller today offers a quick-cooking barley that cuts preparation time to 10 to 12 minutes.

The "pearl" in pearled barley is not a description of grade or quality; it refers to the whiteness and rounded shape of the grain after milling. When harvested, barley grains are enclosed in three-layered husks that are milled away from the kernels, leaving "pearls."

Today, barley is finding its way into dishes that traditionally called for rice, pasta or cracked wheat, such as pilafs, stuffings and salads. Barley Pilaf; Cumin-Coriander Cornish Hens with Barley Stuffing; and Barley, Corn and Cucumber Salad with Tarragon Vinaigrette are just three of the taste treats waiting for you in the pages that follow.

MILLET

Millet may not strike a familiar note in most kitchens, but anyone who has put out a bird feeder or kept a caged bird should know what it is. A good part of the millet grown in this country goes into birdseed mixtures. The millet seeds are the little round shiny ones, usually yellow, sometimes orange-brown. As a food for humans, who eat the grain with its shiny hulls removed, millet was a staple in China before it was displaced by rice, and it's still a major food crop in India and much of Africa.

With 10 to 11 percent protein and good amounts of vitamins and minerals, millet compares favorably with most other cereal grains. In fact, millet offers a greater variety of amino acids than any of the grains commonly consumed in this country. Combined with foods rich in lysine, such as buckwheat or legumes, millet provides protein as useful to the body as the protein in meat, fish or dairy products. As a whole grain, millet has limited kitchen potential because it becomes too soft when cooked for use in salads and the like.

Our Millet Vegetable Soup continues an old southern European tradition of using the grain to thicken hearty soups, while our Birdseed Cookies may just start a new tradition with the delicious crunch they get from whole millet.

RYE

Nowadays rye turns up almost exclusively in commercial baked goods, such as bread, rolls and crackers. Gone are the days when Americans, especially New Englanders, sat down to a big bowl of rye porridge. Gone, too, are the homemade rye pancakes, biscuits, muffins and popovers, but there's nothing stopping us from bringing them back. Rye grows better than wheat in cold, wet climates, hence its early popularity in New England and its continuing favor as a bread grain in northern Europe. The grain's disadvantage in some people's eyes is that rye doughs tend to be sticky, a bit hard to handle, and produce breads that are heavier and denser than those made from wheat.

Rye berries (whole rye kernels) and cracked rye are frequently available at health food stores, and these can be used much like wheat. Rye berries can be sprouted for use in salads and baked products; they can also be cooked and eaten as a breakfast cereal or used in salads. Cracked rye can be added to baked goods, where it provides both flavor and crunch; used to thicken soups, much like barley; or cooked as a hot cereal.

Rye berries and cracked rye usually will keep 1 year or more if stored in airtight containers in a cool, dark place. Rye flours are more perishable. Store for up to 1 month in the cupboard and for 2 to 3 months in the refrigerator.

Barley and Rainbow Sweet Pepper Salad with Garlic Dressing

A rainbow of chopped sweet peppers provides crunch and color to this delightful barley salad. 6 SERVINGS

1½ cups pearled barley
½ medium red bell pepper, chopped
½ medium yellow bell pepper, chopped
½ medium green bell pepper, chopped
3 scallions, chopped
1 carrot, chopped
1 garlic clove, minced
1 teaspoon minced fresh ginger
3 tablespoons canola or corn oil
1 tablespoon Asian sesame oil
2 tablespoons rice wine vinegar
½ teaspoon salt
¼ teaspoon ground pepper

1. In a medium saucepan, heat 3 cups water to boiling over high heat. Add the barley. Reduce the heat to a simmer, cover and cook until tender, about 50 minutes. Drain and let cool.

2. In a large salad bowl, combine the cooked drained barley, the peppers, scallions and carrot.

3. Prepare a dressing by mixing the garlic, ginger, canola oil, sesame oil, vinegar, salt and pepper in a small bowl or by shaking the ingredients together in a jar with a tight-fitting lid. Pour the dressing over the salad and toss until evenly combined.

Calories: 270	Protein: 5 gm	Total Fat: 10 gm
Saturated Fat: 1 gm	Cholesterol: 0 mg	Carbohydrates: 42 gm
Sodium: 193 mg	Dietary Fiber: 9 gm	

A SUPER SOURCE OF:

Vitamin A	████████████████ 84%
Riboflavin	██████ 33%
Vitamin C	██████████ 54%

0%	U.S. Recommended Daily Allowance	100%

An average serving of pearled barley (¼ cup uncooked) contains nearly 8 grams of fiber, including water-soluble fiber, which helps reduce blood cholesterol.

Cumin-Coriander Cornish Hens with Barley Stuffing

Bake any leftover stuffing in this recipe uncovered in the oven as a side dish. It will emerge crisp and crunchy. 4 SERVINGS

½ cup pearled barley
2 teaspoons olive oil, preferably extra virgin
1 medium onion, chopped
1 garlic clove, minced
½ carrot, chopped
½ medium red bell pepper, chopped
¼ cup plus ¼ cup chicken stock or canned low-sodium broth
½ teaspoon salt
¼ teaspoon pepper
2 Cornish hens (1¼ to 1½ pounds each), rinsed and patted dry
2 tablespoons fresh lemon juice
¾ teaspoon cumin
¾ teaspoon coriander

1. In a medium saucepan, heat 1½ cups water to boiling over high heat. Add the barley, reduce the heat, cover and simmer until tender, about 1 hour. Drain and cool.

2. Preheat the oven to 375 degrees. In a medium skillet, heat the oil. Add the onion, garlic, carrot and bell pepper and cook until soft but not brown, about 5 minutes. Set aside.

3. In a large bowl, combine the barley and vegetables. Pour in ¼ cup of the stock. Add the salt and pepper. Mix well. Stuff the hens loosely with the barley mixture and place in a 9-inch square baking dish.

4. In a small bowl, combine the lemon juice, cumin and coriander. Brush over the hens. Pour the remaining ¼ cup stock around the hens in the baking dish. Bake 1¼ hours, or until the juices run clear, basting occasionally with the pan juices.

Calories: 458   Protein: 41 gm   Total Fat: 22 gm
Saturated Fat: 6 gm   Cholesterol: 121 mg   Carbohydrates: 24 gm
Sodium: 400 mg   Dietary Fiber: 5 gm

A SUPER SOURCE OF:

Phosphorus	32%
Vitamin A	66%
Riboflavin	28%
Niacin	66%
Vitamin C	40%

0%   U.S. Recommended Daily Allowance   100%

*B*eef and Barley Soup

On brisk fall days, this hearty soup is a satisfying Sunday supper unto itself. 7 SERVINGS

½ pound flank steak
½ pound beef shank, bone in, trimmed of excess fat
2 cups beef stock or canned low-sodium broth
1 large onion, chopped
1 medium carrot, chopped
1 celery stalk, chopped
1 can (28 ounces) crushed tomatoes, with their juice
⅓ cup pearled barley
2 teaspoons salt
½ teaspoon pepper
2 tablespoons chopped parsley

1. In a large heavy pot, place the flank steak, beef shank and 3 cups water. Bring to a boil. Reduce the heat to a simmer, cover and cook for 1 hour, skimming off the fat occasionally.

2. Add the beef stock, onion, carrot, celery, tomatoes with their juice, barley, salt and pepper. Cook until the meat and barley are tender, about 1 hour.

3. Remove the meat from the pot. Let cool slightly. Discard the bones. Cut the meat into small pieces and return to the pot. Add the parsley and simmer 10 minutes longer.

Calories: 161	Protein: 14 gm	Total Fat: 5 gm
Saturated Fat: 2 gm	Cholesterol: 25 mg	Carbohydrates: 16 gm
Sodium: 862 mg	Dietary Fiber: 3 gm	

A SUPER SOURCE OF:

Vitamin B12	28%
Vitamin A	73%
Niacin	21%
Vitamin C	36%
Zinc	21%

0%   U.S. Recommended Daily Allowance   100%

Pearled barley is the most common choice for soups, stews and other dishes with lengthy cooking times. As a thickener for soup, add about 1 teaspoon of barley for each 1 cup of water or other liquid used in making the broth.

Barley Pilaf

In this country, barley is used chiefly to fatten livestock and make beer, but the grain has long been an important food crop in Middle Eastern and Asian nations. Here barley takes the place of rice in a tasty pilaf. 5 SERVINGS

3 cups chicken stock or canned low-sodium broth
1 cup pearled barley
1 tablespoon safflower oil
3 scallions, chopped
1 celery stalk, chopped
¼ pound mushrooms, sliced
½ teaspoon salt
¼ teaspoon pepper

1. In a medium saucepan, heat the stock to boiling over high heat. Add the barley. Reduce the heat to a simmer, cover and cook until tender, about 50 minutes. Drain and place in a large bowl.

2. In a medium skillet, heat the oil over medium heat. Add the scallions and celery and cook until the celery is crisp-tender, 5 to 6 minutes. Add the mushrooms, salt and pepper and cook until the vegetables are soft and most of the liquid from the mushrooms has evaporated, about 5 minutes.

3. Stir the cooked vegetables into the barley. Mix well. Serve immediately.

Calories: 193	Protein: 6 gm	Total Fat: 4 gm
Saturated Fat: 1 gm	Cholesterol: 0 mg	Carbohydrates: 34 gm
Sodium: 263 mg	Dietary Fiber: 7 gm	

A SUPER SOURCE OF:
Riboflavin ━━━━━━━━ 35%

0%   U.S. Recommended Daily Allowance   100%

Cooked barley can be held in the refrigerator for a day or two before using, or it can be frozen and stored for up to a month.

*W*ild *Mushroom and Barley Soup*

Shiitake and other cultivated "wild" mushrooms are becoming more readily available in supermarkets. Their rich, earthy flavor makes it worth the effort to seek them out. 4 SERVINGS

1 tablespoon safflower oil
2 leeks (white part only), thinly sliced
1 garlic clove, minced
1¼ cups sliced shiitake mushrooms (4 ounces)
1¼ cups sliced white button mushrooms (4 ounces)
4 cups beef stock or canned low-sodium broth
½ cup pearled barley
2 tablespoons chopped fresh dill or 1½ teaspoons dried
¾ teaspoon salt
½ teaspoon ground pepper

1. **In** a large pot, heat the oil over medium heat. Add the leeks and cook until soft but not brown, about 8 minutes. Add the garlic and mushrooms and cook for 5 minutes longer.

2. **Add** the beef stock and stir with a wooden spoon, scraping up any browned bits from the bottom of the pan. Bring to a boil and add the barley. Reduce the heat to a simmer, cover and cook until the barley is tender, about 1 hour.

3. **Add** the dill, salt and pepper and cook 10 minutes longer.

Calories: 163	Protein: 4 gm	Total Fat: 5 gm
Saturated Fat: 0 gm	Cholesterol: 0 mg	Carbohydrates: 28 gm
Sodium: 426 mg	Dietary Fiber: 5 gm	

A SUPER SOURCE OF:
Riboflavin ────── 20%

0%   U.S. Recommended Daily Allowance   100%

Barley, Corn and Cucumber Salad with Tarragon Vinaigrette

Here's another barley salad to try. Fresh tarragon contributes a unique aromatic flavor and is now more readily available at local food markets. Remember, the general rule of substitution for herbs is 3 parts fresh to 1 part dried. 6 SERVINGS

1 cup pearled barley
2 cups cooked corn, fresh or frozen
1 cucumber, peeled, halved lengthwise, seeded and sliced
2 shallots, minced
¼ cup safflower oil
3 tablespoons white wine vinegar
2 garlic cloves, minced
1 tablespoon chopped fresh tarragon or 1 teaspoon dried
½ teaspoon salt
¼ teaspoon pepper

1. In a medium saucepan, heat 3 cups water to boiling over high heat. Add the barley. Reduce the heat to a simmer, cover and cook until tender, about 1 hour. Drain and cool.

2. In a large salad bowl, combine the barley, cooked corn, cucumber and shallots.

3. Prepare a dressing by mixing the oil, vinegar, garlic, tarragon, salt and pepper in a small bowl or by shaking the ingredients together in a jar with a tight-fitting lid. Pour the dressing over the salad and toss.

Calories: 267	Protein: 6 gm	Total Fat: 10 gm
Saturated Fat: 1 gm	Cholesterol: 0 mg	Carbohydrates: 42 gm
Sodium: 197 mg	Dietary Fiber: 7 gm	

A SUPER SOURCE OF:
Riboflavin ████████ 24%

0%   U.S. Recommended Daily Allowance   100%

To prepare 4 cups of cooked barley, bring 4 cups of water or broth to a boil in a large heavy saucepan. Stir in 1 cup medium pearled barley and, if desired, a pinch of salt. Cover, reduce the heat and simmer 45 to 50 minutes.

*B*irdseed Cookies

These delicious little cakes are called "Birdseed Cookies" for good reason: They feature millet, those tiny yellow seeds that are a favorite food of our feathered friends. MAKES 28 COOKIES

½ cup all-purpose flour
½ cup regular or quick-cooking oats
3 tablespoons millet
1 teaspoon baking powder
1 teaspoon cinnamon
½ teaspoon cardamom
¼ cup coarsely chopped dried apricots
4 tablespoons unsalted butter, at room temperature
⅓ cup packed brown sugar
1 egg
1 teaspoon vanilla extract

1. Preheat the oven to 350 degrees. Lightly coat a cookie sheet with vegetable cooking spray.

2. In a medium bowl, combine the flour, oats, millet, baking powder, cinnamon, cardamom and apricots.

3. In another medium bowl, using a hand-held electric mixer or a whisk, cream the butter and brown sugar until light and fluffy, about 3 minutes.

4. Add the egg and vanilla extract and mix until blended. Stir in the dry ingredients just until combined. Drop the batter by heaping teaspoons onto the prepared pan, leaving a 1-inch space between the unbaked cookies.

5. Bake 9 to 11 minutes, or until the cookies are golden and slightly springy to the touch. Remove the cookies from the pan and let cool on a wire rack.

Calories: 49 per cookie	Protein: 1 gm	Total Fat: 2 gm
Saturated Fat: 1 gm	Cholesterol: 12 mg	Carbohydrates: 7 gm
Sodium: 19 mg	Dietary Fiber: .4 gm	

Millet flour can replace up to one fourth the wheat flour in yeast bread recipes and up to half the wheat flour in quick bread, muffin and pancake recipes.

Millet Vegetable Soup

The amino acids in the kidney beans combine with those in the millet to make protein as useful to the body as the protein in meat, fish or dairy products. 4 SERVINGS

1 cup millet
1 tablespoon olive oil
3 scallions, chopped
1 large onion, chopped
2 garlic cloves, minced
3 cups chicken stock or canned low-sodium broth
1 tablespoon tomato paste
1 cup canned red kidney beans, rinsed and drained
1 package (10 ounces) frozen mixed vegetables
1 teaspoon salt
½ teaspoon pepper
¼ cup chopped parsley

1. In a medium saucepan, heat 2 cups water to boiling over high heat. Add the millet. Reduce the heat to low and cook, covered, until the millet is tender and most of the water is absorbed, about 25 to 30 minutes.

2. In a large saucepan, heat the oil. Add the scallions, onion and garlic and cook over medium heat until soft but not brown, about 5 minutes.

3. Add the chicken stock and tomato paste and bring to a boil. Add the beans and mixed vegetables. Reduce the heat to low and simmer, covered, for 15 minutes.

4. Add the salt, pepper, cooked millet and parsley. Cook 5 minutes longer.

Calories: 365	Protein: 14 gm	Total Fat: 8 gm
Saturated Fat: 1 gm	Cholesterol: 0 mg	Carbohydrates: 60 gm
Sodium: 747 mg	Dietary Fiber: 8 gm	

A SUPER SOURCE OF:

Phosphorus	27%
Iron	24%
Vitamin A	89%
Thiamin	25%
Niacin	24%
Vitamin C	37%

0%   U.S. Recommended Daily Allowance   100%

*S*ourdough Rye Bread

The slightly sour taste of this deli-type rye bread comes from the Sourdough Starter. It is not difficult to prepare, but it must be made 2 days in advance of baking, so plan accordingly. The starter will last almost indefinitely as long as it is used and replenished according to the directions below. MAKES 2 LOAVES, 16 SLICES PER LOAF

1⅓ cups warm water (105 to 115 degrees)
1 tablespoon sugar
1 envelope active dry yeast
1 tablespoon salt
2 cups Sourdough Starter—stir before using (recipe follows)
3 tablespoons caraway seeds
2 tablespoons dark molasses
2 cups medium rye flour
3½ to 4 cups bread flour
Cornmeal

1. In a small bowl, place ⅓ cup of the water and the sugar. Stir in the yeast. Let the mixture stand until foamy, about 5 minutes.

2. In a large mixing bowl, place the remaining 1 cup water, the salt and the Sourdough Starter. Add the yeast mixture, caraway seeds, molasses, ½ cup of the rye flour and 2 cups of the bread flour. Using a hand-held electric mixer, beat at medium speed for 2 minutes. Add the rest of the rye flour. Decrease the speed to low and mix 2 minutes longer. Remove the beaters and stir in enough remaining bread flour, ¼ cup at a time, to form a dough that pulls away from the sides of the bowl.

3. Turn the dough out onto a lightly floured surface and knead by hand for 8 to 10 minutes, or until the dough is smooth and shiny. The dough will feel somewhat sticky to the touch.

4. Lightly spray a large bowl with vegetable cooking spray. Place the dough in the bowl and turn to coat evenly. Loosely cover the dough and let rise in a warm draft-free place for 1½ hours, or until it is doubled in size.

5. Punch the dough down and let it rest, covered, for 20 minutes. Lightly coat a large baking sheet with vegetable cooking spray and dust with cornmeal.

6. Lightly flour a wooden board. Divide the dough in half. Shape each half into oval loaves, tapered at the ends. Place the loaves on the prepared baking sheet. Loosely cover with plastic wrap and a slightly dampened kitchen towel and let rise 45 minutes, or until almost doubled in size. Meanwhile, preheat the oven to 400 degrees.

7. Bake the loaves in the preheated oven for 50 minutes, or until the bottoms of the loaves sound hollow when tapped. Remove the loaves from the pan and cool on wire racks.

Calories per slice: 120	Protein: 4 gm	Total Fat: 1 gm
Saturated Fat: 0 gm	Cholesterol: 0 mg	Carbohydrates: 25 gm
Sodium: 108 mg	Dietary Fiber: 1 gm	

Sourdough Starter

MAKES 3 CUPS

3 cups bread flour
1 tablespoon sugar
1 envelope active dry yeast
2 cups warm water (105 to 115 degrees)

1. In a large jar or bowl, combine the flour, sugar and yeast. Gradually add the warm water and mix until smooth.
2. Cover the jar loosely and let it stand at room temperature for 2 days before using. Refrigerate for longer storage.
3. Use as needed according to individual recipes. Replenish the starter by replacing the amount used with equal amounts of flour and warm water. For example, if 2 cups of the starter are used, replace it with 1 cup of flour and 1 cup of water. Re-cover the jar and refrigerate for future use.

On average, rye has a nutritional advantage over wheat. It offers the same nutrients, but usually in greater concentrations. Rye flour averages about 12 percent protein and contains B vitamins, iron, phosphorus and potassium.

Grilled Turkey Salami and Cheese on Rye

This is a favorite lunch or light supper of children and adults alike. Grilled sandwiches are generally very high in fat content. However, using turkey salami and part-skim mozzarella, and baking rather than frying, places this sandwich in the "healthy" category. 4 SERVINGS

8 slices of rye bread
1 tablespoon Dijon mustard
4 slices of tomato
4 ounces turkey salami, sliced
4 ounces part-skim mozzarella, sliced

1. Preheat the oven to 375 degrees. Lightly coat a cookie sheet with vegetable cooking spray.
2. Toast the rye bread in a toaster.
3. Lightly brush the toasted bread with the mustard. Place a slice of tomato on 4 of the slices. Place ¼ of the turkey salami and ¼ of the cheese over the tomatoes. Top with the remaining 4 slices of rye. Press the top of the sandwiches down slightly.
4. Place the sandwiches on the prepared pan. Bake until the sandwiches are heated through and the cheese has melted, about 7 minutes.

Calories: 256	Protein: 16 gm	Total Fat: 10 gm
Saturated Fat: 4 gm	Cholesterol: 29 mg	Carbohydrates: 28 gm
Sodium: 688 mg	Dietary Fiber: 3 gm	

A SUPER SOURCE OF:

Calcium ▬▬▬ 23%
Phosphorus ▬▬▬ 21%

0%   U.S. Recommended Daily Allowance   100%

*R*ye Caraway Pancakes

These hearty flapjacks feature rye as a main grain. Dotted with caraway seeds, it's reminiscent of deli rye bread. 5 SERVINGS

1 cup rye flour
¾ cup all-purpose flour
2 tablespoons caraway seeds
1 tablespoon baking powder
½ teaspoon salt
1 whole egg
2 egg whites
2 tablespoons safflower oil
1¾ cups buttermilk

1. Lightly coat a large skillet or griddle with vegetable cooking spray.
2. In a large bowl, combine the rye flour, all-purpose flour, caraway seeds, baking powder and salt.
3. In a medium bowl, mix the whole egg, egg whites, oil and buttermilk. Add all at once to the dry ingredients. Stir just until combined. The batter should be slightly lumpy.
4. Drop about 3 tablespoons of the batter onto the prepared skillet for each pancake. Cook over medium heat until golden on the bottom with small bubbles on the top, about 3 to 4 minutes. Turn and cook until golden on the other side, about 2 minutes. Serve immediately.

Calories: 257
Saturated Fat: 1 gm
Sodium: 600 mg

Protein: 10 gm
Cholesterol: 46 mg
Dietary Fiber: 3 gm

Total Fat: 8 gm
Carbohydrates: 36 gm

A SUPER SOURCE OF:

Calcium	━━━━━━	26%
Phosphorus	━━━━━	21%
Riboflavin	━━━━━	21%

0%   U.S. Recommended Daily Allowance   100%

To make rye porridge, stir 1 part cracked rye into 3 parts boiling water in a heavy saucepan. Reduce the heat, cover and simmer about 40 minutes.

Rye Buttermilk Dill Batter Bread

Three grains are combined to make this dense loaf. Simple to assemble, it's wonderful fresh from the oven or sliced and toasted.

MAKES 1 LOAF, 16 SLICES

1½ cups all-purpose flour
1 cup rye flour
½ cup oat bran cereal
1 tablespoon sugar
2 teaspoons baking powder
1 teaspoon baking soda
½ teaspoon salt
1 tablespoon chopped fresh dill or 1 teaspoon dried
1½ cups buttermilk
¼ cup safflower oil
1 egg

1. Preheat the oven to 375 degrees. Lightly coat a 9 × 5 × 3–inch loaf pan with vegetable cooking spray.
2. In a large mixing bowl, combine the all-purpose flour, rye flour, oat bran, sugar, baking powder, baking soda, salt and dill.
3. In a medium bowl, whisk the buttermilk, oil and egg. Add the liquid ingredients all at once to the dry ingredients. Stir only until moistened; the batter should be slightly lumpy. Spread into the prepared pan.
4. Bake 50 minutes, or until a toothpick inserted in the center comes out clean. Let cool in the pan on a wire rack for 5 minutes. Remove the loaf from the pan and finish cooling on the wire rack.

Calories: 101 per slice
Saturated Fat: 1 gm
Sodium: 201 mg

Protein: 3 gm
Cholesterol: 14 mg
Dietary Fiber: 1 gm

Total Fat: 4 gm
Carbohydrates: 12 gm

Boston Brown Bread

MAKES 2 LOAVES, 12 SLICES PER LOAF

1 cup yellow cornmeal
1 cup rye flour
1 cup whole wheat flour
1 teaspoon baking powder
1 teaspoon baking soda
¼ teaspoon salt
½ cup raisins
2 cups buttermilk
½ cup molasses

1. Lightly coat two 1-pound coffee cans with vegetable cooking spray. Place a wire rack on the bottom of a large stockpot or roasting pan with a tight-fitting lid. Cut 2 pieces of string 24 inches long. Remove the lid and fill the pot with enough hot water to reach halfway up the sides of the empty cans. Tear off two 6-inch pieces of aluminum foil and lightly coat with vegetable cooking spray.

2. In a large bowl, place the cornmeal, rye flour, whole wheat flour, baking powder, baking soda, salt and raisins. Stir to mix.

3. In a medium bowl, blend the buttermilk and molasses. Add all at once to the dry ingredients. Stir only until moistened; the batter should be slightly lumpy.

4. Pour the batter evenly into the prepared coffee cans. Cover with the pieces of aluminum foil, pressing the sides of the foil to the outsides of the cans. Tie tightly with the string. Steam over low heat, covered, for 1¾ to 2 hours, adding more water if necessary to keep the level constant. Cut the strings and remove the foil carefully. Insert toothpicks in the centers of each loaf. If they come out clean, the breads are done. Remove the cans from the pot and let cool for 10 minutes on a dry wire rack. Unmold the breads from the cans and cool 30 minutes before serving.

Calories per slice: 88	Protein: 2 gm	Total Fat: 1 gm
Saturated Fat: 0 gm	Cholesterol: 1 mg	Carbohydrates: 19 gm
Sodium: 98 mg	Dietary Fiber: 2 gm	

One ounce (about ¼ cup) of dark rye flour provides 92 calories from 19 grams carbohydrate, 5 grams protein and less than 1 gram fat.

Mixed Grain Bread Sticks

Bread sticks are fun to bake. Try poppy seeds or minced onion flakes if you prefer them to the sesame seeds called for in this version. MAKES 20 BREAD STICKS

1¼ cups warm water (105 to 115 degrees)
2 teaspoons sugar
1 envelope active dry yeast
2 tablespoons safflower oil
2 cups bread flour
¾ cup whole wheat flour
¾ cup rye flour
1 teaspoon salt
Cornmeal
1 egg white, beaten
¼ cup sesame seeds

1. In a large mixing bowl, combine the warm water and sugar. Stir in the yeast. Let stand until foamy, about 5 minutes. Mix in the oil.
2. Add 1 cup of the bread flour, all of the whole wheat and rye flours and the salt to the yeast mixture. Using a hand-held electric mixer, beat at medium speed for 2 minutes. Decrease the speed to low and mix 2 minutes longer. With a wooden spoon, stir in enough remaining bread flour, ¼ cup at a time, to form a dough that pulls away from the sides of the bowl.
3. Turn the dough out onto a lightly floured surface and knead by hand for 8 to 10 minutes, or until the dough is smooth and elastic.
4. Lightly spray a large bowl with vegetable cooking spray. Place the dough in the bowl and turn to coat evenly. Cover the dough and let rise in a draft-free area 1 hour, or until doubled in size.
5. Divide the dough into 20 pieces. Roll and stretch each piece into a rope. Lightly coat a rimmed cookie sheet with vegetable cooking spray and dust with cornmeal. Place the sticks on the prepared baking sheet, leaving a space between each. Cover and let the dough rise 30 minutes, or until almost doubled in size. Meanwhile, preheat the oven to 400 degrees.
6. Brush the bread sticks lightly with the beaten egg white and sprinkle with the sesame seeds. Bake 20 minutes, or until they are golden brown and sound hollow when tapped. Remove them from the pan and cool on a wire rack.

Calories: 105 per bread stick   Protein: 3 gm   Total Fat: 3 gm
Saturated Fat: 0 gm   Cholesterol: 0 mg   Carbohydrates: 17 gm
Sodium: 114 mg   Dietary Fiber: 1 gm

Amaranth, Buckwheat and Quinoa

Buckwheat

When Mark Twain got homesick while visiting Europe in the 1870s, one thing he longed for was buckwheat cakes and maple syrup. To the author of *Huckleberry Finn*, this was American food at its finest, and he wasn't alone in that belief.

Buckwheat cakes were once much more popular than they are today. We even immortalized them in the words to "Oh, Susannah," which has had generations of schoolchildren and summer campers singing how "the buckwheat cake was in her mouth" without the foggiest notion why. Tastes changed, however, and buckwheat's popularity declined. Now with renewed interest in healthy eating and grains, perhaps buckwheat is ripe for a comeback.

Buckwheat is one of a small group of grains that isn't produced by a cereal grass. The plant is related to rhubarb and garden sorrel and has little white or pink-tinted flowers. In fact, the part of the plant we eat isn't even a seed, as it is in cereal grains; it's a tiny fruit. Technicalities aside, buckwheat has been used as a grain for centuries—hulled and cooked into porridge or ground into flour used mostly for griddle cakes. In Central and eastern Europe, hulled buckwheat grains are called "kasha."

Noodles made from buckwheat are popular in Japan. Called "soba," these are the basis of our unusual and savory Buckwheat Noodles in Spicy Peanut Sauce.

The "Supergrains"

Amaranth and quinoa are two more grains that come from plants other than cereal grasses. Amaranth is the seed of a plant related to the tumbleweed of the American Southwest. Quinoa (pronounced "keen-WAH") comes from a plant distantly related to spinach, Swiss chard and beets. In fact, the leaves of the quinoa plant can be cooked and eaten like spinach.

Amaranth and quinoa have been hailed as "supergrains" and are slowly gaining popular attention. They're called "supergrains" because they're high in protein and because the protein they contain is special. The proteins in grains always lack one or more of the eight amino acids, the building blocks of proteins that humans must have in their diet. Quinoa and amaranth offer a more complete variety of amino acids than other grains.

What may seem surprising is that these wonder grains are anything but new. Health food enthusiasts have known about them for decades, botanists for upward of a century, and natives of South and Central America for thousands of years. Found growing wild in Mexico and regions to the south, amaranth was the principal grain crop of the Aztecs; quinoa, indigenous to Chile, was the grain of the Incas. The two have similar nutritional profiles, but are very different in flavor and texture.

AMARANTH

Amaranth seeds, often called "grain amaranth," are the shape and color and about one eighth the size of white mustard seeds. High in fiber and very rich in iron, amaranth contains as much as 16 percent protein, including the amino acids lysine and methionine, which are mostly absent from the seeds of cereal grasses. Vegetarians combine amaranth with whole wheat or corn to produce a protein as useful to the body as the protein in meat.

Amaranth cooks into a thick porridge that's somewhat sweet and calls to mind flavors like beets. The uncooked grain, lightly toasted in a dry skillet, makes a nice topping for salads and cooked noodles. Amaranth flour can be substituted for up to one quarter of the wheat flour in yeast bread recipes and up to half the wheat flour in quick bread, muffin and pancake recipes.

QUINOA

Quinoa seeds are tiny, about the size and color of coarse sand. Like amaranth, the grain can contain as much as 16 percent protein and is rich in vitamins and minerals. Combined with buckwheat, which is high in the amino acid lysine, it provides complete protein, just like meat, fish or dairy products.

Of the two "supergrains," quinoa has the greater culinary potential. The grain is delicately flavored and fluffy when cooked and can be substituted in many dishes calling for rice, bulgur or couscous. When preparing quinoa, be sure you first put the amount of grain you want in a fine sieve, rinse it with cold running water and drain it thoroughly. Otherwise, the grain will be bitter.

Quinoa contains a good deal of oil and so does quinoa flour, which adds a tender moistness to baked goods enriched with it. Quinoa flour can be substituted for up to one fourth of the wheat flour in yeast bread recipes and up to half the wheat flour in quick bread, muffin and pancake recipes.

> *Several plants related to amaranth are grown in flower gardens. Two are showy plants with showy names: love-lies-bleeding and prince's feather.*

Buckwheat Almond Waffles

Buckwheat and almonds bolster each other to give these low-fat waffles plenty of nutty flavor. 5 SERVINGS

1 cup buckwheat flour
1 cup all-purpose flour
2 teaspoons baking powder
½ teaspoon baking soda
¼ teaspoon salt
2 tablespoons safflower oil
1¾ cups buttermilk
1 whole egg
2 egg whites
2 tablespoons honey
¼ cup coarsely chopped almonds

1. Preheat a waffle iron and lightly coat with vegetable cooking spray.

2. In a large bowl, combine the buckwheat flour, all-purpose flour, baking powder, baking soda and salt.

3. In a medium bowl, combine the oil, buttermilk, whole egg, egg whites, honey and almonds. Add to the dry ingredients and stir until just blended; the batter should be slightly lumpy.

4. Pour about ⅓ cup of the batter onto the prepared waffle iron and cook about 4 to 5 minutes, or until the waffle is golden brown and crisp. Repeat with the remaining batter. Serve the waffles immediately with fresh fruit or a drizzle of maple syrup.

Calories: 341	Protein: 12 gm	Total Fat: 12 gm
Saturated Fat: 2 gm	Cholesterol: 46 mg	Carbohydrates: 49 gm
Sodium: 487 mg	Dietary Fiber: 4 gm	

A SUPER SOURCE OF:

Calcium	22%
Phosphorus	26%
Thiamin	21%
Riboflavin	26%

0%   U.S. Recommended Daily Allowance   100%

> The name buckwheat derives from German words meaning "beech wheat," a reference to the fact that buckwheat grains are pyramid-shaped, like beechnut kernels, and are put to the same kinds of uses as wheat.

Buckwheat Silver Dollars

Buckwheat flour gives these minipancakes a nutlike flavor, and the walnuts contribute a crunchy texture. 5 SERVINGS

1¼ cups all-purpose flour
½ cup buckwheat flour
1 tablespoon baking powder
¼ teaspoon salt
2 tablespoons chopped walnuts
1 whole egg
2 egg whites
2 tablespoons safflower oil
1 tablespoon maple syrup
1½ cups skim milk

1. Lightly coat a large skillet or griddle with vegetable cooking spray.

2. In a large bowl, combine the all-purpose flour, buckwheat flour, baking powder, salt and walnuts.

3. In a medium bowl, combine the whole egg, egg whites, oil, maple syrup and skim milk. Whisk until blended. Add all at once to the dry ingredients. Stir only until moistened; the batter should be slightly lumpy.

4. Drop heaping tablespoons of the batter onto the prepared skillet. Cook the pancakes over medium heat until golden on the bottom with small bubbles on the top, about 3 minutes. Turn and cook until lightly browned on the other side, about 2 minutes. Serve immediately.

Calories: 280	Protein: 10 gm	Total Fat: 9 gm
Saturated Fat: 1 gm	Cholesterol: 44 mg	Carbohydrates: 40 gm
Sodium: 438 mg	Dietary Fiber: 2 gm	

A SUPER SOURCE OF:

Calcium	▬▬▬▬	24%
Phosphorus	▬▬▬	21%
Thiamin	▬▬▬	21%
Riboflavin	▬▬▬	22%

0%   U.S. Recommended Daily Allowance   100%

*B*uckwheat Noodles in Spicy Peanut Sauce

Cold noodles with sesame or peanut sauce are a Chinese take-out favorite. Here this tasty dish is easily made with buckwheat noodles and peanut butter. The results are delicious and, what's more, the amino acids in the peanuts and noodles combine to make a complete protein. 5 SERVINGS

8 ounces Japanese buckwheat noodles (soba)
2 tablespoons peanut butter
2 tablespoons reduced-sodium soy sauce
1 tablespoon peanut oil
2 teaspoons Asian sesame oil
2 tablespoons rice wine vinegar
2 teaspoons honey
½ teaspoon ginger
⅛ teaspoon crushed hot pepper flakes
¼ teaspoon ground pepper
1 garlic clove, minced
3 scallions, chopped

1. In a large saucepan of boiling water, cook the noodles until tender, about 8 minutes. Scoop out and reserve 2 tablespoons of the cooking liquid. Drain the noodles.

2. In a medium bowl, combine the peanut butter, reserved noodle cooking liquid, soy sauce, peanut oil, sesame oil, vinegar, honey, ginger, hot pepper flakes, ground pepper and garlic. Whisk until blended.

3. Place the noodles in a large bowl. Pour the sauce over the noodles and toss until evenly combined. Sprinkle the scallions over the top. Serve at room temperature.

Calories: 248   Protein: 9 gm   Total Fat: 8 gm
Saturated Fat: 1 gm   Cholesterol: 0 mg   Carbohydrates: 39 gm
Sodium: 631 mg   Dietary Fiber: 1 gm

A SUPER SOURCE OF:
Niacin   ▬▬▬▬▬▬▬▬▬▬▬▬ 78%

       0%   U.S. Recommended Daily Allowance   100%

Buckwheat, Tuna and Artichoke Salad

Buckwheat, usually served hot, stands up to the assertive flavors of artichokes and capers in this offbeat but delicious grain salad.

5 SERVINGS

1 cup medium buckwheat groats
1 egg white
1 teaspoon salt
2 cups boiling water
2 tablespoons olive oil
1 tablespoon fresh lemon juice
1 tablespoon tarragon vinegar or white wine vinegar
1 tablespoon Dijon mustard
½ teaspoon tarragon
3 scallions, chopped
1 tablespoon capers
¼ teaspoon pepper
*1 box (10 ounces) frozen artichoke hearts, cooked and
    drained*
¼ pound mushrooms, sliced
*1 can (7 ounces) water-packed solid white tuna, drained
    and flaked*

1. In a medium saucepan, combine the buckwheat, egg white and ½ teaspoon of the salt. Cook over medium-high heat, stirring, until the grains are separate, about 5 minutes. Pour the boiling water slowly and carefully over the buckwheat; it will splatter. Reduce the heat to low and simmer, covered, until the buckwheat is tender and the liquid is absorbed, about 15 minutes. Place in a large bowl and let cool.

2. Prepare a dressing by whisking together the olive oil, lemon juice, vinegar, mustard, tarragon, scallions, capers, the remaining ½ teaspoon salt and the pepper in a small bowl or by shaking the ingredients together in a jar with a tight-fitting lid.

3. Add the cooked artichoke hearts, mushrooms and tuna to the buckwheat. Pour the dressing over the salad and toss until coated.

Calories: 249	Protein: 17 gm	Total Fat: 8 gm
Saturated Fat: 1 gm	Cholesterol: 16 mg	Carbohydrates: 31 gm
Sodium: 540 mg	Dietary Fiber: 7 gm	

A SUPER SOURCE OF:
Niacin ▬▬▬▬ 26%

0%   U.S. Recommended Daily Allowance   100%

Sweet Peppers Stuffed with Buckwheat, Spinach and White Beans

In Europe, spinach and white beans are frequently served to-gether as a side dish. Here they're partnered with buckwheat groats and rice bran as a filling for sweet red bell peppers. 6 SERVINGS

3/4 cup medium buckwheat groats
1 egg white
1 1/2 teaspoons salt
1 1/2 cups boiling water
6 large red bell peppers
1 tablespoon safflower oil
3 shallots, chopped
1 garlic clove, minced
1 pound fresh spinach leaves, washed well and drained, or
    1 box (10 ounces) frozen spinach, thawed and drained
1/2 cup canned white cannellini beans, rinsed and drained
1/2 cup rice bran
1/4 teaspoon pepper
1/2 cup chicken stock or canned low-sodium broth

1. Preheat the oven to 350 degrees. Lightly coat a 9-inch square baking dish large enough to hold the peppers upright with vegetable cooking spray.

2. In a medium saucepan, combine the buckwheat, egg white and 1/2 teaspoon of the salt. Cook over medium-high heat, stirring, until the grains are separate, about 5 minutes. Pour the boiling water slowly and carefully over the buckwheat; it will splatter. Reduce the heat to low and simmer, covered, until the buckwheat is tender and the liquid is absorbed, about 15 minutes. Place in a large bowl and let cool.

3. Core each pepper and cut a thin slice from the top.

4. In a large noncorrosive skillet, heat the oil over medium heat. Add the shallots and garlic and cook until soft but not brown, about 3 minutes. Add the spinach and cook until it is wilted and the liquid evaporates, about 4 to 5 minutes. Stir in the beans. Cook 2 minutes longer.

5. **Add** the vegetables to the buckwheat. Mix in the rice bran, pepper and remaining 1 teaspoon salt. Mix well. Lightly stuff each pepper with the buckwheat mixture. Place the peppers into the prepared pan. Pour the stock around the peppers. Bake 20 minutes, or until the peppers can be easily pierced with the tip of a knife.

Calories: 179	Protein: 8 gm	Total Fat: 5 gm
Saturated Fat: 1 gm	Cholesterol: 0 mg	Carbohydrates: 31 gm
Sodium: 497 mg	Dietary Fiber: 9 gm	

A SUPER SOURCE OF:

Phosphorus	25%
Iron	29%
Vitamin A	100%
Thiamin	25%
Niacin	23%
Vitamin C	100%

0%   U.S. Recommended Daily Allowance   100%

A 1-ounce serving (approximately ⅓ cup) of rice bran provides 90 calories from 14 grams of carbohydrates, 4 grams of protein and 6 grams of fat.

Beef, Kasha and Lima Bean Soup

This meat and soup combination is a wonderful hearty meal for a cold winter night. The meat can be removed from the broth, broiled and eaten with some of the beans. The kasha is put into soup plates and served with the soup. 6 SERVINGS

½ pound dry large lima beans
1 pound beef shanks, trimmed of excess fat
1 pound meaty soup bones
1 medium onion
2 carrots, sliced
2 celery stalks
1½ teaspoons salt
½ teaspoon pepper
1 cup medium buckwheat groats (kasha)
1 egg white
2 cups boiling water

1. Place the lima beans in a large saucepan. Add enough water to cover by 2 inches. Bring to a boil over high heat. Remove the pan from the heat, cover and let the beans soak for 1 hour; drain.

2. Return the beans to the pot and add 3 cups of water. Bring to a boil over high heat. Add the beef shanks and meaty bones and return to a boil, skimming as necessary. Add the onion, carrots, celery, salt and pepper. Reduce the heat to a simmer, cover and cook until the meat and beans are tender, 1½ to 2 hours.

3. Meanwhile, in a medium saucepan, combine the kasha and egg white. Cook over medium-high heat, stirring, until the grains are separate, about 5 minutes. Pour the boiling water slowly and carefully over the kasha; it will splatter. Reduce the heat to low and simmer, covered, until the kasha is tender and the liquid is absorbed, about 15 minutes. Set aside.

4. Remove the meat, bones, onion and celery stalks from the pot. Preheat the broiler. Place the beef shanks on a broiler rack. Broil until brown and crisp on top, 5 to 6 minutes. Turn and broil until brown and crisp on the other side, 5 to 6 minutes.

5. To serve, place about ½ cup of the kasha into each soup bowl. Add the soup, some of the beans and the sliced carrots. Serve the broiled beef and the rest of the beans separately on plates.

Calories: 340	Protein: 29 gm	Total Fat: 4 gm
Saturated Fat: 1 gm	Cholesterol: 30 mg	Carbohydrates: 48 gm
Sodium: 636 mg	Dietary Fiber: 12 gm	

A SUPER SOURCE OF:

Phosphorus	41%
Iron	31%
Vitamin B12	42%
Vitamin A	100%
Thiamin	23%
Niacin	33%
Zinc	47%

0%   U.S. Recommended Daily Allowance   100%

A 1-ounce portion of uncooked buckwheat (about ⅓ cup) provides 94 calories from 20 grams of carbohydrates, 3 grams of protein and less than 1 gram of fat.

Brisket of Beef with Kasha and Mushrooms

Slow gentle cooking turns lean brisket into a deliciously tender main course. Here it is served with kasha and sautéed mushrooms.
7 SERVINGS.

2 pounds first-cut brisket of beef, well trimmed
1 garlic clove, thinly sliced
1 tablespoon plus 2 teaspoons safflower oil
1 large onion, sliced
2 cups beef stock or canned low-sodium broth
1 cup dry red wine
¾ teaspoon salt
¼ teaspoon pepper
½ pound mushrooms, sliced
1 cup medium buckwheat groats (kasha)
1 egg white
2 cups boiling water

1. With a small sharp knife, cut vertical slits, about ¾ inch deep, into the surface of the meat. Insert the garlic slices into the slits.

2. In a large flameproof casserole, heat 1 tablespoon of the oil over medium-high heat. Add the brisket and cook until well browned on the bottom, 8 to 10 minutes. Turn the meat over and cook until brown on the other side, about 6 minutes. Add the onions and cook, stirring, until they begin to color, 6 to 8 minutes.

3. Pour in the stock and wine. Bring to a boil, stirring and scraping the browned bits from the bottom of the pan. Add ½ teaspoon of the salt and the pepper. Reduce the heat to a simmer, cover and cook, skimming off the fat occasionally, for 2 to 2½ hours, or until the brisket is tender.

4. In a large skillet, heat the remaining 2 teaspoons oil over medium-high heat. Add the mushrooms and cook until most of the liquid has evaporated, about 5 minutes.

5. In a medium saucepan, combine the kasha, egg white and the ¼ teaspoon salt. Cook over medium-high heat, stirring, until the grains are separate, about 5 minutes. Add the cooked mushrooms. Pour the boiling water slowly and carefully over the kasha; it will splatter. Reduce the heat to a simmer and cook, covered, until the kasha is tender and the liquid is absorbed, about 15 minutes.

6. Transfer the brisket to a cutting board and let rest for 15 minutes. Pour the pan juices into a small bowl. Thinly slice the beef across the grain. Spoon the kasha and mushrooms onto a large serving platter. Arrange the sliced beef over the kasha. Degrease the pan juices. Spoon some over the brisket and kasha. Pass the rest separately.

Calories: 323	Protein: 32 gm	Total Fat: 12 gm
Saturated Fat: 3 gm	Cholesterol: 77 mg	Carbohydrates: 22 gm
Sodium: 347 mg	Dietary Fiber: 4 gm	

A SUPER SOURCE OF:

Phosphorus	40%
Iron	20%
Vitamin B12	52%
Riboflavin	27%
Niacin	41%
Zinc	36%

0%   U.S. Recommended Daily Allowance   100%

Hungarian Goulash Soup with Buckwheat

7 SERVINGS

1 cup medium buckwheat groats
1 egg white
2 cups boiling water
1 tablespoon safflower oil
2 medium onions, chopped
1 green bell pepper, chopped
2 garlic cloves, minced
1 tablespoon paprika, preferably Hungarian sweet
1 teaspoon caraway seeds
1 can (28 ounces) crushed tomatoes, with their juice
3 cups beef stock or canned low-sodium broth
1 pound round steak, cut into 1-inch cubes
1½ teaspoons salt
½ teaspoon pepper
1 cup nonfat plain yogurt
1 tablespoon minced fresh chives or 1 teaspoon dried

1. In a medium saucepan, combine the buckwheat and egg white.
Cook over medium-high heat, stirring, until the grains are separate,
about 5 minutes. Pour the boiling water slowly and carefully over
the buckwheat; it will splatter. Reduce the heat to low and simmer,
covered, until the buckwheat is tender, about 15 minutes. Set aside.

2. In a large saucepan, heat the oil over medium heat. Add the
onions, bell pepper and garlic and cook until very soft, 6 to 8
minutes. Add the paprika and caraway seeds. Cook, stirring, 2
minutes longer.

3. Add the tomatoes with their liquid and the stock. Bring to a
boil over high heat. Add the round steak, salt and pepper. Reduce
the heat to a simmer, cover and cook, skimming as necessary, until
the beef is tender, 1½ to 2 hours.

4. In a small bowl, combine the yogurt and chives. To serve, place
about ⅓ cup of the buckwheat in each soup bowl. Add some of the
soup and meat. Top with a dollop of chive yogurt.

Calories: 256	Protein: 21 gm	Total Fat: 7 gm
Saturated Fat: 1 gm	Cholesterol: 38 mg	Carbohydrates: 30 gm
Sodium: 737 mg	Dietary Fiber: 4 gm	

A SUPER SOURCE OF:

Phosphorus	30%
Vitamin B12	35%
Vitamin A	28%
Niacin	25%
Vitamin C	58%
Zinc	23%

0%　　　U.S. Recommended Daily Allowance　　　100%

Carrot Buckwheat Popovers

Carrot pairs with nutty buckwheat in these lighter-than-air popovers. This not-too-sweet version contains a fraction of the fat found in traditional popovers. MAKES 12 POPOVERS

1 medium carrot, peeled and coarsely chopped
1 whole egg
2 egg whites
1¼ cups buttermilk
3 tablespoons melted unsalted butter
1 cup buckwheat flour
¼ cup packed brown sugar
1 teaspoon cinnamon
½ teaspoon nutmeg

1. Preheat the oven to 400 degrees. Lightly coat a 12-count muffin tin with vegetable cooking spray.

2. In a blender, combine the carrot, whole egg, egg whites, buttermilk and melted butter. Process until thoroughly mixed. Add the buckwheat flour, brown sugar, cinnamon and nutmeg and blend until just combined.

3. Pour the batter into the prepared muffin pan. Bake 35 minutes, or until the popovers are puffed and golden. Turn out and serve immediately.

Calories: 99 per popover	Protein: 3 gm	Total Fat: 4 gm
Saturated Fat: 2 gm	Cholesterol: 26 mg	Carbohydrates: 14 gm
Sodium: 45 mg	Dietary Fiber: 1 gm	

A SUPER SOURCE OF:
Vitamin A ━━━━━━━━━ 37%

0%   U.S. Recommended Daily Allowance   100%

Buckwheat Rye Rolls

These whole-grain rolls are dense in texture, with a deep hearty flavor. Characteristically, they do not rise as high as yeast products made with bread flour only. Using a food processor to blend the dough and knead it at the same time makes these scratch rolls a snap. MAKES 8 ROLLS

1 cup plus 2 tablespoons warm water (105 to 115 degrees)
1 tablespoon honey
2 envelopes active dry yeast
2⅓ cups bread flour
½ cup buckwheat flour
½ cup rye flour
1 teaspoon salt
Cornmeal
1 egg white, lightly beaten

1. In a small bowl, combine the warm water and honey. Stir in the yeast. Let the mixture stand until foamy, about 5 minutes.

2. In a food processor fitted with the metal blade, place 2 cups of the bread flour, all of the buckwheat and rye flours and the salt. With the machine on, add the yeast mixture through the feed tube. When it begins to form a ball, process 45 seconds longer, until the dough is smooth. If the dough is too wet and doesn't form a ball, add the remaining ⅓ cup bread flour, 1 tablespoon at a time.

3. Lightly spray a large bowl with vegetable cooking spray. Place the dough in the bowl and turn to coat evenly. Loosely cover the dough and let rise in a warm draft-free place for 1½ hours, or until it is doubled in size.

4. Lightly flour a wooden board. Coat a cookie sheet with vegetable cooking spray and dust with cornmeal. Divide the dough into 8 equal pieces. Shape each piece into a smooth ball. Flatten slightly. Place the rolls onto the prepared baking sheet, leaving a 2-inch space between each. Cover loosely with plastic wrap and a slightly damp kitchen towel. Let the rolls rise 45 minutes. They will not double in size. Meanwhile, preheat the oven to 400 degrees.

5. Brush the tops of the rolls with the beaten egg white. Bake 18 to 20 minutes, until the rolls sound hollow when tapped on the bottom.

Calories per roll: 209	Protein: 7 gm	Total Fat: 1 gm
Saturated Fat: 0 gm	Cholesterol: 0 mg	Carbohydrates: 42 gm
Sodium: 284 mg	Dietary Fiber: 2 gm	

A SUPER SOURCE OF:

| Thiamin | ———— 27% |
| Niacin | ———— 21% |

0%   U.S. Recommended Daily Allowance   100%

Sweet Buckwheat Crepes with Brandied Apple Sauce

Buckwheat gives these crepes a nutty flavor. Folded and topped with sweet cooked apples and brandy, they make a very special dessert. 6 SERVINGS

⅔ cup all-purpose flour
⅓ cup buckwheat flour
¼ teaspoon salt
3 tablespoons sugar
3 teaspoons cinnamon
¾ cup skim milk
1 whole egg
2 egg whites
2 tablespoons safflower oil
3 large tart-sweet apples such as Granny Smith, peeled and cut into ½-inch dice
¼ cup unsweetened apple juice
2 tablespoons applejack or Calvados

1. In a blender or food processor, combine the all-purpose flour, buckwheat flour, salt, 1 tablespoon sugar, 1 teaspoon cinnamon, milk, 1 cup water, whole egg, egg whites and oil. Blend on high speed until well blended. Let the batter rest for 30 minutes.

2. In a medium saucepan over medium heat, cook the apples, apple juice and remaining 2 tablespoons sugar and 2 teaspoons cinnamon until the apples are just tender, about 10 minutes. Add the applejack and cook 5 minutes longer. Set the brandied apple sauce aside.

3. Lightly spray an 8-inch crepe pan or frying pan with sloping sides with vegetable cooking spray. Heat the pan over medium-high heat to very hot.

4. Pour about 3 tablespoons of the crepe batter into the hot pan and swirl to cover the bottom. Cook until the bottom of the crepe is golden and the edges begin to darken, 3 to 4 minutes. Turn over and cook until the other side is spotted brown, 30 to 60 seconds. Slide the crepe out of the pan and onto a paper towel to absorb any excess moisture. Repeat the procedure until all the batter is used.

5. Preheat the oven to 350 degrees. Lightly coat an 8½ × 11–inch baking dish with vegetable cooking spray. Fold each cooked crepe in half and then into quarters. Place in the prepared baking dish. Spoon the sauce decoratively over the crepes. Bake until hot, about 10 minutes. Allow 3 crepes per serving.

Calories: 237	Protein: 6 gm	Total Fat: 6 gm
Saturated Fat: 1 gm	Cholesterol: 36 mg	Carbohydrates: 39 gm
Sodium: 135 mg	Dietary Fiber: 3 gm	

*H*ot Buckwheat with Raisins and Apricots

Raisins and apricots lend flavor and a touch of sweetness to this comforting breakfast cereal. 4 SERVINGS

1 cup skim milk
¼ teaspoon salt
¾ cup fine buckwheat groats
3 tablespoons honey
1 teaspoon cinnamon
¼ cup raisins
2 tablespoons chopped dried apricots

1. In a medium saucepan, combine the milk, salt and 1½ cups water. Bring to a boil over high heat.

2. Stir in the buckwheat until mixed. Add the honey and cinnamon. Reduce the heat to medium-low.

3. Stir in the raisins and apricots. Cover and simmer for 15 minutes, or until the liquid is absorbed.

Calories: 214	Protein: 6 gm	Total Fat: 1 gm
Saturated Fat: 0 gm	Cholesterol: 1 mg	Carbohydrates: 49 gm
Sodium: 173 mg	Dietary Fiber: 5 gm	

*T*urkey Quinoa Vegetable Soup

Quinoa, one of the oldest grains known, cooks up very quickly. To avoid a trace of bitterness, make sure to rinse the grain well before using. 7 SERVINGS

1 tablespoon safflower oil
1 medium onion, chopped
1 celery stalk, chopped
1 green bell pepper, chopped
4 cups chicken stock or canned low-sodium broth
½ cup quinoa, rinsed well and drained
1 package (10 ounces) frozen mixed vegetables
½ pound cooked turkey breast, cut into ½-inch chunks
¼ cup chopped parsley
1 teaspoon sage
2 teaspoons salt
½ teaspoon pepper

1. In a large saucepan, heat the oil. Add the onion, celery and bell pepper. Cook over medium heat until soft but not brown, about 5 minutes.

2. Pour in the stock and 2 cups water. Bring to a boil. Add the quinoa. Reduce the heat to low, cover and cook until the quinoa is almost tender, about 12 minutes.

3. Add the mixed vegetables, turkey, parsley, sage, salt and pepper. Cook 10 minutes longer.

Calories: 168	Protein: 14 gm	Total Fat: 8 gm
Saturated Fat: 1 gm	Cholesterol: 22 mg	Carbohydrates: 16 gm
Sodium: 714 mg	Dietary Fiber: 2 gm	

A SUPER SOURCE OF:

Vitamin A ———————— 45%
Niacin ———— 20%
Vitamin C —————— 35%

0%   U.S. Recommended Daily Allowance   100%

A 1-ounce serving of uncooked quinoa provides 106 calories from 20 grams of carbohydrates, 4 grams of protein and 2 grams of fat.

Smothered Chicken with Quinoa

Chicken is surrounded by aromatic vegetables and all are simmered in stock flavored by sherry. The quinoa cooks up quickly, right in the same pot, soaking up the delicious juices. 4 SERVINGS

1 tablespoon safflower oil
2 medium onions, chopped
2 carrots, sliced
1 celery stalk, sliced
1 garlic clove, minced
1 pound skinless, boneless chicken breasts, cut into 1-inch chunks
1½ cups chicken stock or canned low-sodium broth
½ cup dry sherry
¾ cup quinoa, rinsed well and drained
1 teaspoon thyme leaves
½ teaspoon salt
¼ teaspoon pepper

1. In a large skillet, heat the oil over medium heat. Add the onions, carrots, celery and garlic and cook until soft but not brown, about 5 minutes. Push the vegetables to the sides of the pan. Increase the heat to medium-high. Add the chicken and cook, tossing frequently, until lightly browned outside and white to the center, 6 to 8 minutes.

2. Add the stock and sherry. Bring to a boil. Reduce the heat to low and cook, covered, 10 minutes.

3. Add the quinoa, thyme, salt and pepper. Cook 15 minutes, or until the quinoa is tender and has absorbed some of the liquid.

4. Serve the chicken, vegetables, quinoa and remaining juices in soup bowls.

Calories: 333	Protein: 32 gm	Total Fat: 7 gm
Saturated Fat: 1 gm	Cholesterol: 66 mg	Carbohydrates: 34 gm
Sodium: 412 mg	Dietary Fiber: 6 gm	

A SUPER SOURCE OF:

Phosphorus	39%
Iron	28%
Vitamin A	100%
Niacin	73%

0%   U.S. Recommended Daily Allowance   100%

Crunchy Quinoa Salad

East meets West in this savory salad, which combines Chinese-style seasonings with vegetables that originated in Europe and a South American grain. 6 SERVINGS

½ cup quinoa
1 cup boiling water
1 head of romaine lettuce, torn into bite-size pieces
1 celery stalk, chopped
1 cucumber, peeled and sliced
3 radishes, thinly sliced
1 carrot, chopped
1 can (8 ounces) sliced water chestnuts, drained
2 scallions, chopped
1 garlic clove, minced
1 teaspoon minced fresh ginger
¼ cup chopped fresh cilantro or parsley
¼ cup corn oil
2 tablespoons fresh lemon juice
2 teaspoons reduced-sodium soy sauce
½ teaspoon salt
¼ teaspoon pepper

1. Rinse the quinoa well under cold running water; drain. In a medium saucepan of boiling water, cook the quinoa over low heat, covered, until tender, about 15 minutes. Drain and let cool.

2. In a large salad bowl, combine the quinoa, lettuce, celery, cucumber, radishes, carrot, water chestnuts and scallions.

3. Prepare a dressing by whisking together the garlic, ginger, cilantro, oil, lemon juice, soy sauce, salt and pepper in a small bowl or by shaking the ingredients together in a jar with a tight-fitting lid. Pour the dressing over the salad and toss until coated.

Calories: 184	Protein: 4 gm	Total Fat: 10 gm
Saturated Fat: 1 gm	Cholesterol: 0 mg	Carbohydrates: 20 gm
Sodium: 282 mg	Dietary Fiber: 4 gm	

A SUPER SOURCE OF:

Vitamin A ████████████████████████ 100%
Vitamin C ████████████████ 57%

0%   U.S. Recommended Daily Allowance   100%

Quinoa's nutty flavor can be enhanced by first browning the seeds for about 5 minutes in a dry or lightly oiled skillet.

*A*maranth in Tomato-Wine Sauce with Carrots and Onions

Amaranth was cultivated by the Aztecs at least 5,000 years ago. It is a hardy plant that withstands anything nature has to offer. Loaded with protein, it can be cooked in liquid or popped like corn in small quantities. 4 SERVINGS

1 cup dry red wine
1 cup no-salt-added tomato sauce
1 cup amaranth
1 tablespoon safflower oil
1 onion, chopped
1 carrot, chopped
1 garlic clove, minced
¼ cup chopped parsley
½ teaspoon salt
¼ teaspoon pepper

1. In a medium saucepan, heat the wine and tomato sauce to boiling over high heat. Add the amaranth. Reduce the heat to a simmer, cover and cook until the amaranth is tender, 22 to 25 minutes. Remove the cover and stir. The consistency will be creamy. Remove from the heat, cover again and set aside.

2. In a medium skillet, heat the oil. Add the onion, carrot and garlic and cook over medium heat until softened, about 5 minutes. Stir in the parsley, salt and pepper and cook 2 minutes longer.

3. Add the vegetables to the amaranth. Stir to combine.

Calories: 254	Protein: 8 gm	Total Fat: 7 gm
Saturated Fat: 1 gm	Cholesterol: 0 mg	Carbohydrates: 41 gm
Sodium: 307 mg	Dietary Fiber: 9 gm	

A SUPER SOURCE OF:

Phosphorus	25%
Iron	27%
Vitamin A	100%
Vitamin C	30%

0%   U.S. Recommended Daily Allowance   100%

Leftover cooked amaranth can be spread over the bottom of an oiled baking dish and chilled overnight. The next morning, cut into squares or wedges and fry in a little oil, much as you might cold grits.

FOR FINICKY EATERS

You can see it coming and it isn't a pretty sight: You tell your little prehistorians that Mediterranean Vegetable Bulgur Salad is what baby dinosaurs always ate, and you don't make a fuss when more of it goes into the family brontosaurus (long-haired dachshund) than into their little tummies. And you don't wince when they won't even look at the Vegetable Couscous with Chick-Peas you lovingly prepare a week later. . . .

Why put yourself through all that? You're really disinclined to risk mass extinction of your patience, aren't you? And there is an easier way: Start your family on the road to survival of the fittest with our special recipes for kids. Our Pita Pizzas are guaranteed to keep little pterodactyls soaring; our Oat Meatball Soup with Whole Wheat Elbows will satisfy the hungriest tyrannosaurus.

Seriously, getting children to eat right is sometimes challenging, but finding the right recipe is usually more than half the battle. During their growth years, children need proportionately greater amounts of nourishment than adults. Pound for pound, a child aged 1 to 3 years needs more than six times as much iron as a man aged 25 to 50, six times as much phosphorus, one and a half times the protein and more than twice as much thiamin, riboflavin and niacin—all substances abundant in grain and grain products.

The recipes in this section take the approach of using ingredients that are fun and familiar as a way of introducing the less familiar. If there were a kid seal of approval, these recipes would have it.

Our Tamale Pie combines corn, ground turkey, crushed tomatoes and cheese for a savory, easy-to-make supper. Peanut Butter and Oat Fruit Bars can be popped into a lunchbox or stuffed into a pocket. The Banana Crunch Pudding Parfaits add the goodness of wheat germ to a sinfully delicious dessert.

By the way, should a hungry dinosaur turn up in your kitchen, try serving her some of our Cocoa Applesauce Muffins. They've been known to please other fearsome critters.

*P*eanut Butter and Oat Fruit Bars

Here every kid's favorite sandwich is transformed into a dessert. Any kind of fruit spread will do if black cherry isn't a first choice.

MAKES 16 BARS

¾ cup regular or quick-cooking oats
¾ cup all-purpose flour
¼ cup whole wheat flour
2 teaspoons baking powder
⅓ cup packed brown sugar
⅛ teaspoon salt
⅓ cup peanut butter
¼ cup peanut oil
1 cup buttermilk
½ teaspoon almond extract
1 whole egg
2 egg whites
⅓ cup black cherry fruit spread or other low-sugar spread

1. Preheat the oven to 350 degrees. Lightly coat an 8-inch square baking pan with vegetable cooking spray.

2. In a large bowl, combine the oats, all-purpose flour, whole wheat flour, baking powder, brown sugar and salt. Set the dry ingredients aside.

3. In a medium bowl, place the peanut butter, oil, buttermilk, almond extract, whole egg and egg whites. Whisk until well blended. Add the dry ingredients and mix just until combined.

4. Spread the batter into the prepared pan. Drop the fruit spread by tablespoons onto the batter in the pan. With a knife, swirl the fruit through the batter, creating a marbled effect. Bake 30 to 35 minutes, or until a toothpick inserted in the center of the cake comes out clean. Cool the cake in the pan on a wire rack. Cut into 2-inch squares.

Calories per bar: 148	Protein: 4 gm	Total Fat: 7 gm
Saturated Fat: 1 gm	Cholesterol: 14 mg	Carbohydrates: 18 gm
Sodium: 124 mg	Dietary Fiber: 1 gm	

Chicken Soup with Rice

Both your mother and Maurice Sendak, author of *Chicken Soup with Rice* (published by Harper & Row), knew about the virtues of this comforting broth. He concluded this children's favorite book with the following:

I told you once
I told you twice
all seasons
of the year
are nice
for eating
chicken soup
with rice!*

5 SERVINGS

1 cup long-grain white rice
1 pound chicken breasts, skinned, bone in
2 carrots, cut into 1-inch pieces
2 celery stalks with leaves, halved
1 medium onion
2 sprigs of fresh dill (optional)
¼ cup sprigs of fresh parsley
1½ teaspoons salt
½ teaspoon pepper

1. In a medium saucepan, bring 2 cups water to a boil over high heat. Add the rice. Reduce the heat to a simmer, cover and cook until the rice is tender and the water is absorbed, 18 to 20 minutes.

2. In a large saucepan, place the chicken, carrots, celery, onion, dill, parsley, salt and pepper. Bring to a boil over high heat. Reduce the heat to a simmer, cover and cook, skimming the surface occasionally, until the chicken is tender, about 45 minutes.

3. Discard the celery, onion, dill and parsley. Remove the chicken from the bones. Cut the meat into small pieces and return to the pot. Add the rice and simmer 2 minutes. Serve hot.

Calories: 217	Protein: 17 gm	Total Fat: 1 gm
Saturated Fat: 0 gm	Cholesterol: 34 mg	Carbohydrates: 34 gm
Sodium: 717 mg	Dietary Fiber: 2 gm	

A SUPER SOURCE OF:

Vitamin A ————————————————— 100%
Niacin ——————— 42%

0%   U.S. Recommended Daily Allowance   100%

*From *Chicken Soup with Rice* by Maurice Sendak. Copyright © 1962 by Maurice Sendak. Reprinted by permission of HarperCollins Publishers.

*T*omato and Rice Soup with Mixed Vegetables

Many of us were raised on canned cream of tomato soup with rice. Here's a lean tomato-rice soup made even healthier with the addition of mixed vegetables. 6 SERVINGS

½ cup long-grain white rice
3 cups chicken stock or canned low-sodium broth
2 cups canned crushed tomatoes, with their juice
1 cup frozen mixed vegetables
1 tablespoon chopped parsley
½ teaspoon salt
¼ teaspoon pepper

1. In a medium saucepan, heat 1 cup water to boiling over high heat. Add the rice. Reduce the heat to a simmer, cover and cook until the rice is tender and the water is absorbed, 18 to 20 minutes. Drain and reserve.

2. In a large saucepan, combine the chicken stock and tomatoes with their liquid. Bring to a boil.

3. Stir in the mixed vegetables. Reduce the heat and simmer 5 minutes. Add the cooked rice, parsley, salt and pepper and cook 2 minutes longer.

Calories: 109	Protein: 4 gm	Total Fat: 1 gm
Saturated Fat: 0 gm	Cholesterol: 0 mg	Carbohydrates: 21 gm
Sodium: 355 mg	Dietary Fiber: 1 gm	

A SUPER SOURCE OF:
Vitamin A ━━━━━━━━━ 41%
Vitamin C ━━━━━ 26%

0%   U.S. Recommended Daily Allowance   100%

*T*una *Cheese Melt*

Anything with cheese in it has a certain amount of saturated fat. To keep such fat at a minimum in this favorite with the youngsters, be sure to use part-skim mozzarella and try to find rye bagels that have been made with water only and contain no egg. 4 SERVINGS

4 rye water bagels, halved lengthwise
2 tablespoons nonfat plain yogurt
1 tablespoon reduced-calorie no-cholesterol mayonnaise
1 teaspoon Dijon mustard
1 can (7 ounces) water-packed tuna, drained
¼ cup shredded carrot
4 slices tomato
¼ cup grated part-skim mozzarella cheese

1. Preheat the oven to 375 degrees. Lightly coat an 8-inch square baking pan with vegetable cooking spray.

2. Toast the bagel halves in a toaster.

3. In a small bowl, combine the yogurt, mayonnaise and mustard. Blend well.

4. In a medium bowl, place the tuna. Stir in the yogurt mixture. Add the carrot.

5. Place the toasted bagel halves on the prepared pan. Spread with ¼ of the tuna mixture. Top each with a slice of tomato and sprinkle with the grated cheese. Bake until the sandwiches are heated through and the cheese has melted, about 2 to 3 minutes.

Calories: 249	Protein: 21 gm	Total Fat: 4 gm
Saturated Fat: 1 gm	Cholesterol: 23 mg	Carbohydrates: 32 gm
Sodium: 566 mg	Dietary Fiber: not available	

A SUPER SOURCE OF:
Vitamin A ━━━━━━━━ 42%

0%   U.S. Recommended Daily Allowance   100%

*O*ven-Baked Fish Sticks

4 SERVINGS

2 teaspoons safflower oil
2 egg whites
⅓ cup oat bran
⅓ cup yellow cornmeal
1 tablespoon chopped parsley
½ teaspoon salt
¼ teaspoon pepper
1 pound mild-flavored white fish fillets, such as cod or
  haddock, cut ½ inch thick
Lemon wedges (optional)

1. Preheat the oven to 400 degrees. Lightly coat a cookie sheet with vegetable cooking spray.

2. In a small bowl, combine the oil and egg whites. Whisk until blended. In a shallow dish, mix together the oat bran, cornmeal, parsley, salt and pepper.

3. Cut the fish into 3 × 1–inch sticks. Dip the fish into the egg white mixture. Pat all sides lightly with the dry ingredients. Place the coated fish sticks onto the prepared pan.

4. Bake for 10 minutes. Turn the fish over and bake 10 minutes longer, or until golden brown. Serve the fish sticks hot with lemon wedges, if desired.

Calories: 183	Protein: 24 gm	Total Fat: 4 gm
Saturated Fat: 0 gm	Cholesterol: 49 mg	Carbohydrates: 14 gm
Sodium: 363 mg	Dietary Fiber: 2 gm	

A SUPER SOURCE OF:

Phosphorus ━━━━━━━ 30%
Vitamin B12 ━━━━━ 18%

0%   U.S. Recommended Daily Allowance   100%

Pita Pizza

Traditional pizza toppings on toasted pitas are a quick and delicious way to feed your family. And kids love them. 4 SERVINGS

2 whole wheat pita breads, about 6 inches in diameter
(p. 26), split into 2 thin rounds each
1 cup Chunky Tomato Sauce (p. 54)
½ cup grated part-skim mozzarella cheese
¼ cup grated Parmesan cheese
1 tablespoon chopped parsley
½ teaspoon dried oregano
½ teaspoon dried basil

1. Preheat the oven to 350 degrees. Lightly coat a large baking pan with vegetable cooking spray. Place halved pitas on the prepared pan. Bake until crunchy and toasted, about 10 minutes. Remove the pan from the oven.

2. Spread ¼ of the Chunky Tomato Sauce over each toasted pita half. Sprinkle both cheeses over the sauce, dividing evenly.

3. In a small bowl, combine the parsley, oregano and basil. Sprinkle the herbs over the cheese topping. Bake until the sauce is hot and the cheese is bubbly, about 5 minutes.

Calories: 175 Protein: 9 gm Total Fat: 5 gm
Saturated Fat: 3 gm Cholesterol: 12 mg Carbohydrates: 23 gm
Sodium: 580 mg Dietary Fiber: 3 gm

A SUPER SOURCE OF:

Calcium ———— 21%
Vitamin A ————————— 64%
Vitamin C ———— 21%

0%   U.S. Recommended Daily Allowance   100%

*O*at Meatball Soup with Whole Wheat Elbows

This is one tasty way to feed your children their meat, vegetables and pasta and do it with a single pot. Broiling the meatballs first eliminates excess fat and seals in flavor. 4 SERVINGS

¾ pound very lean ground beef
1 small onion, grated
¼ cup regular or quick-cooking oats
¼ cup plus 1 tablespoon chopped fresh parsley
4 cups chicken stock or canned low-sodium broth
2 cups no-salt-added tomato juice
2 celery stalks, chopped
1 box (10 ounces) frozen mixed vegetables
½ cup whole wheat elbow macaroni
¼ teaspoon pepper

1. Preheat the broiler. Lightly coat an 8-inch square baking pan with vegetable cooking spray.

2. In a medium bowl, combine the beef, onion, oats, 2 tablespoons of water and 1 tablespoon of parsley. Mix the ingredients to blend well. Shape into balls about ¾ inch in diameter. Place the meatballs on the prepared pan and broil about 4 inches from the heat until brown on top, 5 to 6 minutes. Turn the meatballs over and broil on the other side until brown, about 4 minutes. Drain the meatballs on paper towels.

3. In a medium saucepan, combine the stock and tomato juice. Bring to a boil. Add the meatballs, reduce the heat to low, cover and cook for 15 minutes.

4. Add the celery, mixed vegetables and macaroni. Cook 10 minutes, or until the macaroni is just tender. Add the remaining ¼ cup chopped parsley and the pepper. Cook 2 minutes longer.

Calories: 336	Protein: 25 gm	Total Fat: 13 gm
Saturated Fat: 5 gm	Cholesterol: 53 mg	Carbohydrates: 31 gm
Sodium: 164 mg	Dietary Fiber: 3 gm	

A SUPER SOURCE OF:

Phosphorus	23%
Iron	27%
Vitamin A	91%
Niacin	36%
Vitamin C	60%

0%   U.S. Recommended Daily Allowance   100%

*T*amale Pie

Kids love Mexican food, and using a small amount of polyunsaturated oil and lean ground turkey instead of beef makes this as healthy as it is tasty. 7 SERVINGS

3 cups chicken stock or canned low-sodium broth
¾ cup yellow cornmeal
½ teaspoon salt
1 tablespoon safflower or vegetable oil
1 medium onion, chopped
1 garlic clove, minced
1 pound very lean ground turkey
2 cups canned crushed tomatoes, with their juice
¼ cup tomato paste
1 tablespoon chili powder
1 teaspoon oregano
½ teaspoon cumin
1 cup fresh or frozen corn kernels
2 tablespoons canned mild chopped green chiles
2 tablespoons grated Parmesan cheese

1. Lightly coat a 2½-quart casserole with vegetable cooking spray.

2. In a large saucepan, combine ¾ cup of the chicken stock with the cornmeal and salt. In a medium saucepan, bring the remaining 2¼ cups stock to a boil. Stir the boiling hot stock into the cornmeal. Reduce the heat to a simmer, cover and cook, stirring occasionally, until the mixture thickens, about 10 minutes.

3. In a large noncorrosive skillet, heat the oil over medium heat. Add the onion and garlic and cook until soft but not brown, about 5 minutes. Add the ground turkey. Cook, stirring to break up lumps, until the meat loses its pink color, about 7 minutes.

4. Preheat the oven to 375 degrees. Add the tomatoes with their juice, tomato paste, chili powder, oregano and cumin to the skillet. Reduce the heat to low, cover and simmer for 15 minutes. Stir in the corn and chiles.

5. Spoon the cooked cornmeal into the prepared pan, spreading to the edges with a rubber spatula. Evenly ladle the turkey filling over the cornmeal. Sprinkle the cheese over the top. Bake until the cornmeal layer is firm and the cheese is golden, about 20 minutes.

Calories: 234	Protein: 16 gm	Total Fat: 9 gm
Saturated Fat: 2 gm	Cholesterol: 48 mg	Carbohydrates: 23 gm
Sodium: 482 mg	Dietary Fiber: 3 gm	

A SUPER SOURCE OF:

Vitamin A	━━━━ 24%
Niacin	━━━━ 25%
Vitamin C	━━━━ 32%

0%   U.S. Recommended Daily Allowance   100%

Stromboli with Cheese and Eggplant Filling

Cornmeal pizza dough, made in a jiffy in a food processor, is filled with sautéed eggplant, onions and garlic, topped with two kinds of cheese, then rolled and baked. The result is a meal in itself, something the kids can just pick up and enjoy. 6 SERVINGS

1 cup warm water (105 to 115 degrees)
2 teaspoons sugar
1 envelope active dry yeast
2⅓ cups bread flour
1 cup white cornmeal
1 teaspoon salt
2 tablespoons olive oil, preferably extra virgin
1 small eggplant, peeled and cut into ½-inch dice
1 small onion, chopped
1 garlic clove, minced
½ cup Chunky Tomato Sauce (p. 54)
3 ounces part-skim mozzarella cheese, shredded
¼ cup grated Parmesan cheese
Cornmeal
1 egg white, lightly beaten

1. In a small bowl, place the water and sugar. Stir in the yeast. Let the mixture stand until foamy, about 5 minutes.

2. In a food processor fitted with the metal blade, place 2 cups of the bread flour, the cornmeal and the salt. With the machine on, add the yeast mixture and 1 tablespoon olive oil through the feed tube. When it forms a ball, process 45 seconds longer, or until the dough is smooth and elastic. If the dough is too wet and doesn't form a ball, gradually add the remaining ⅓ cup of bread flour, 1 tablespoon at a time.

3. Lightly spray a large bowl with vegetable cooking spray. Place the dough in the bowl and turn to coat evenly. Loosely cover the dough and let rise in a warm draft-free place for 1 hour, or until it is doubled in size.

4. While the dough is rising, prepare the filling. In a large skillet, heat the remaining 1 tablespoon olive oil over medium heat. Add the eggplant, onion and garlic and cook, stirring occasionally, until soft, 6 to 8 minutes. Add the Chunky Tomato Sauce and ¼ cup of water. Cook 10 minutes, or until the vegetables are very soft and most of the liquid has evaporated. Remove the pan from the heat and let cool.

5. **O**n a lightly floured surface, roll out the risen dough into a 12 × 18–inch rectangle. Spoon the filling in a strip 2 inches from one of the long sides, leaving a 2-inch border at both short edges as well. Sprinkle the mozzarella and Parmesan cheeses over the eggplant filling. Roll up the long side closest to the filling to enclose it. Turn in both short sides and continue rolling to the edge. Pinch the seam to seal. Lightly coat a large cookie sheet with vegetable cooking spray and dust with cornmeal. Transfer the roll, seam side down, onto the prepared pan. Loosely cover and let the filled dough rise 45 minutes, or until almost doubled in size. Preheat the oven to 400 degrees.

6. **B**rush the top of the dough with the egg white. Bake 25 to 30 minutes, or until the crust is golden brown and the bottom sounds hollow when tapped. Remove the loaf from the pan and let cool slightly on a wire rack. Cut into ¾-inch slices and serve warm.

Calories: 409	Protein: 15 gm	Total Fat: 10 gm
Saturated Fat: 3 gm	Cholesterol: 11 mg	Carbohydrates: 65 gm
Sodium: 588 mg	Dietary Fiber: 2 gm	

A SUPER SOURCE OF:

Phosphorus	━━━━	21%
Iron	━━━━	21%
Vitamin A	━━━━	23%
Thiamin	━━━━━━━	41%
Riboflavin	━━━━━	28%
Niacin	━━━━━	29%

0%   U.S. Recommended Daily Allowance   100%

*P*ear Oatmeal Bars

Pears have a natural sweetness, but they are not used as often as apples in baked desserts. Try this tasty bar and perhaps you'll become a fancier of this versatile fruit. MAKES 16 SQUARES

4 medium pears, peeled and cut into ½-inch dice
¼ cup pear nectar or apple juice
1 teaspoon vanilla extract
½ teaspoon almond extract
2 teaspoons cornstarch
1 cup all-purpose flour
½ cup regular or quick-cooking oats
¼ cup sugar
1½ teaspoons cinnamon
½ teaspoon nutmeg
4 tablespoons unsalted butter, cut into ½-inch slices, softened
2 tablespoons slivered almonds

1. **P**reheat the oven to 350 degrees. Lightly coat an 8-inch square baking pan with vegetable cooking spray.

2. **I**n a medium saucepan, place the pears, pear nectar and ¼ cup water. Cook over medium-low heat, stirring occasionally, until the pears are crisp-tender, 3 to 5 minutes. Add the vanilla and almond extract.

3. **I**n a small bowl, dissolve the cornstarch in 2 tablespoons cold water. Stir into the pears. Bring to a boil, stirring until slightly thickened, about 1 minute. Transfer the mixture to the prepared baking pan.

4. **I**n a medium bowl, combine the flour, oats, sugar, cinnamon and nutmeg. Cut in the butter with a pastry blender or 2 knives until the mixture is crumbly and the consistency of coarse meal. Sprinkle over the pears in the pan. Scatter the slivered almonds on top.

5. **B**ake 30 to 35 minutes, until the pears are tender and the topping is golden. Set the pan on a wire rack and let cool completely before cutting into 2-inch squares.

Calories per bar: 112	Protein: 2 gm	Total Fat: 4 gm
Saturated Fat: 2 gm	Cholesterol: 8 mg	Carbohydrates: 18 gm
Sodium: 1 mg	Dietary Fiber: 2 gm	

Cocoa Applesauce Muffins

Cocoa has much less fat than other forms of chocolate and, paired here with applesauce, produces a moist, fudgy, guiltless treat. MAKES 12 MUFFINS

1¼ cups all-purpose flour
½ cup oat bran
⅓ cup sugar
¼ cup unsweetened cocoa powder
2 teaspoons baking powder
½ teaspoon baking soda
¼ teaspoon salt
1 cup buttermilk
¼ cup safflower oil
½ cup unsweetened applesauce
1 whole egg
2 egg whites
1 teaspoon vanilla extract

1. Preheat the oven to 375 degrees. Line a 12-count muffin tin with paper baking cups.
2. In a large bowl, combine the flour, oat bran, sugar, cocoa, baking powder, baking soda and salt.
3. In a medium bowl, place the buttermilk, oil, applesauce, whole egg, egg whites and vanilla. Whisk until well blended. Add all at once to the dry ingredients. Stir only until moistened; the batter should be slightly lumpy.
4. Spoon the batter evenly into the prepared pan. Bake 20 to 25 minutes, or until the muffins are golden and springy to the touch. Remove the muffins from the pan and let cool on a wire rack.

Calories per muffin: 146	Protein: 9 gm	Total Fat: 6 gm
Saturated Fat: 1 gm	Cholesterol: 19 mg	Carbohydrates: 21 gm
Sodium: 187 mg	Dietary Fiber: 2 gm	

*B*anana Crunch Pudding Parfaits

This dessert has the contrasting textures of smooth and crunchy in every mouthful. Peaches or blueberries are worthy alternatives to the bananas. 4 SERVINGS

⅓ cup wheat germ
2 tablespoons packed brown sugar
½ teaspoon cinnamon
1 large banana, sliced
2 tablespoons fresh lemon juice
1 recipe Vanilla Cornstarch Pudding (recipe follows)

1. In a small bowl, combine the wheat germ, brown sugar and cinnamon. Set aside.

2. In a small bowl, toss the banana slices with the lemon juice to prevent discoloration.

3. Pour half of the Vanilla Cornstarch Pudding into 4 custard cups. Drain the banana slices and divide among the custard cups, placing the slices over the pudding. Sprinkle half of the wheat germ mixture over the sliced bananas. Cover with the remaining pudding and sprinkle with the rest of the wheat germ mixture. Refrigerate the parfaits until cold, at least 2 hours.

Calories: 227	Protein: 7 gm	Total Fat: 1 gm
Saturated Fat: 0 gm	Cholesterol: 2 mg	Carbohydrates: 48 gm
Sodium: 136 mg	Dietary Fiber: 2 gm	

A SUPER SOURCE OF:
Phosphorus ━━━━━━━ 24%

0%   U.S. Recommended Daily Allowance   100%

Vanilla Cornstarch Pudding

This updated pudding uses skim milk and less sugar than some of the older versions of vanilla pudding. SERVES 4

2 cups skim milk
3 tablespoons cornstarch
⅓ cup sugar
⅛ teaspoon salt
1 teaspoon vanilla extract

1. In a medium saucepan, cook 1½ cups of the milk over medium heat until very hot and bubbles appear around the sides of the pan.

2. In a small bowl, combine the remaining ½ cup of milk with the cornstarch, sugar and salt. Whisk until smooth.

3. Stir the cornstarch mixture into the hot milk. Bring to a boil, stirring frequently. Cook, whisking, until thick and smooth, 2 to 3 minutes. Stir in the vanilla and stir until blended. Pour the hot pudding into a bowl or individual custard cups. Cover the pudding directly with waxed paper to prevent a skin from forming. Refrigerate until cold, at least 2 hours.

INDEX